THE I^3 LEADER

Leading Authentically as the Same Person in Every Room

DR. ALICIA PARTEE

The I^3 Leader: Leading Authentically as the Same Person in Every Room

Published by Authentigrate

Library of Congress Control Number: [To be assigned]

ISBN: 979-8-9856663-7-3 (hardcover)

ISBN: 979-8-9856663-6-6 (paperback)

ISBN: 979-8-9856663-8-0 (ebook)

Cover design by Muhammad Usman

Interior design by Muhammad Usman

First Edition: March or April 2026

10 9 8 7 6 5 4 3 2 1

Printed in the United States of America

For Tyrone...
...who has seen every version of me
and chose the whole one.

For my mother Patricia...
...my first mirror, my fiercest protector.

For every leader who has been told
they were too much in one room
and not enough in another.

You are allowed to be whole.

The deepest fatigue is not physical. It is the quiet erosion that happens when you keep editing yourself to belong.

~ **Alicia Partee**

CONTENTS

FOREWORD
CYNTHIA D. JAMES, PH.D., D.MIN.

The I^3 Leader: Leading Authentically as the Same Person in Every Room is essential reading. This book is nearly beyond description in terms of its unique value and practical applications because it is a masterclass in authentic leadership on the global stage that offers tools for leaders to strengthen identity, expand influence, and have consistent authentic identity. In an era defined by interconnectedness and cultural complexity, the demand for leadership that is both effective and authentic has never been greater. *The I^3 Leader* is a guide, a seminal text, and a resonant manifesto for all multicultural leaders. It bridges the inner journey of self-discovery and the practical outer journey of contextual influence, and it provides a coherent, actionable, and deeply insightful roadmap.

The foundational brilliance of the manuscript lies in its treatment of identity. It moves beyond simplistic, check-the-box categories to explore identity as a dynamic, layered, and powerful source of strength. Alicia Partee deftly guides readers through the process of reflective excavation and helps them distinguish between the inherited, the adopted, and the essential self. It's not about choosing a single aspect of one's identity over another; it is about integrating multiple strands into a cohesive, confident whole. This leads to the development of a stable core from which all leadership emanates. Each section of the book sharpens cultural assessment and clarifies values. The strategies for decision making and navigating ambiguous global environments are both sophisticated and immediately applicable. Using this toolkit, leaders may amplify their voices and extend their impact.

The book rightly and wisely argues that authenticity is the consistent application of one's core values across varying contexts—not static self-expression. The game-changer is that it permanently resolves the issue of code-switching versus compromise, reframing adaptability as a strength rooted in integrity. The specific examples inspire and serve as a powerful validation of the manuscript's thesis.

The I^3 Leader is a triumph of leadership thought. Its prose is eloquent and accessible. The structure is logical and cumulative—each chapter builds on the previous chapter. The tone is consistently professional, empathetic, and empowering. Ascending leaders, seasoned executives and even their next-door neighbors can renew the impact of their own agency and ability to guide with greater authenticity.

Most books about leadership fill a niche, but *The I^3 Leader* carves out new territory. It is an unforgettable work that is transformative, easy to read, and is urgently needed in a society where human authenticity is increasingly important.

I strongly recommend this book without reservation as a stand-alone best read to anyone courageous enough to present their authentic self in all endeavors.

Cynthia D. James, PhD., D.Min.
Landmark Ministries Inc., President

FOREWORD
BY ANN HEIGHT

Leadership today is being tested. Not by a lack of intelligence or ambition, but by a lack of integration. Across Silicon Valley, elsewhere in American corporate culture, and in organizations around the globe, the pace of change has outgrown leadership models built on assimilation, self-editing, and borrowed authority. What is being asked of leaders now is something more demanding and more sustainable: to lead from a unified sense of identity, grounded in integrity, and expressed through meaningful impact.

This is the work Alicia Partee has been advancing for years.

I have lived and worked across cultures, in the United States, Jamaica, and Canada. I have experienced culture shock and the quieter, often more unsettling experience of reverse culture shock. Each transition required me to consciously remember who I was in environments that subtly, and sometimes overtly, suggested I should adapt by becoming someone else. I have been in rooms and on boards where I was the only woman of color, where difference was apparent before a single word was spoken.

In those moments, identity was not theoretical, it was anchoring. Knowing who I was gave me presence. It allowed me to lead with clarity rather than defensiveness, and with conviction rather than performance.

I tried, briefly, to lead as I was told I should. It was exhausting. I learned quickly that fragmentation carries a high cost. Leading as myself was easier, not because it was effortless, but because it was honest. I didn't have to manage versions of myself or remember which parts to bring into the room. Alignment created energy. And that energy translated into better decisions, stronger relationships, and greater impact.

This is the problem *The I^3 Leader* addresses so clearly.

Alicia's framework recognizes that leadership is not sustainable when identity is disconnected from action, or when integrity is treated as situational rather than foundational. *The I^3 Leader* offers leaders a way to identify who they are, how they choose to show up, and how they integrate. It does not ask leaders to soften their strength or dilute their conviction. It asks them to lead from coherence.

What distinguishes this book is its insistence that integration is not a one-time insight, but a lived practice. The 90-Day Integration Posture is a powerful example of this. Rather than prescribing quick fixes or performative change, Alicia provides readers with a structured, intentional period to observe, align, and act. This posture creates space for reflection without paralysis and action without reactivity. It builds confidence, clarity, and trust, both internally and across teams, by allowing readers to lead deliberately, not defensively.

I have seen what becomes possible when leaders operate from this integrated posture. Authenticity, while sometimes uncomfortable at first, opens the door to hidden capacities, creativity, intuition, and innovation that cannot emerge under the weight of self-editing. Organizations become more adaptive. Cultures become more inclusive. Performance becomes more sustainable.

The I^3 Leader is an invitation, to stop working so hard at being acceptable and start leading from what is true. It is a bold statement for this moment—the future of leadership belongs to those who are integrated, intentional, and grounded in who they are.

As you read this book, I invite you to consider where greater integration might be asking for your attention. Not as a critique, but as a possibility. What might shift for you, for your team, for your organization, if you chose to lead from identity, guided by integrity, toward lasting impact?

This book does not simply meet the moment. It prepares you for what comes next.

Ann Height
Business Advisor

INTRODUCTION
FROM FRAGMENTATION TO INTEGRATION

I was standing in a dark bathroom of my home in Norway, gripping the edge of a cold sink, staring at a reflection I no longer recognized.

The woman looking back at me had credentials. She previously led teams at Fortune 500 companies, built systems during the chaos of the dot-com era, pastored congregations through transition, earned licenses, degrees, and recognition. She had crossed cultures, entered rooms where she was unexpected, and found her footing through intelligence, adaptability, and sheer discipline. She knew how to perform and deliver. She knew how to read any room and respond with care.

And none of it was working anymore.

I moved to Norway to support my husband's work, preparing the way high-capacity leaders do through research, planning, and carefully mapped logistics. I learned the transportation system, studied the culture, and anticipated the challenges. Friends assured me I would be fine, and I agreed.

However, the reality is that preparation can organize logistics, but it can't protect identity.

After months of editing myself to fit into a culture that couldn't read me, I began erasing identifying words on my LinkedIn profile—pastor and therapist—because a well-meaning friend said my background looked "crazy," and another person whose approval I wanted told me I wasn't learning Norwegian fast enough.

So, there I stood, staring at myself in a bathroom mirror when I finally asked the only question that mattered: "Who am I?"

Not what did I do. Not where did I belong. Not what was I supposed to accomplish here.

That question didn't rise from despair. It rose from disorientation. The strategies that carried me across every environment finally stopped working. I was not failing in any measurable way, but I was unraveling. I realized, standing there in the cold Norwegian darkness that I couldn't perform my way through this transition without losing myself in the process.

Living in Norway didn't introduce me to fragmentation. It exposed it.

Long before that international move, my life had been marked by adaptation. I learned early on how to read environments, adjust my presence, and deliver what each room required. At work, one posture. At home, another. In faith spaces, another. Across cultures, other postures—as needed.

Each environment rewarded a particular expression of me, and over time, I became skilled at calibrating which version was needed.

Society has several words for that behavior: emotional intelligence, professionalism, and cultural competence.

But there is a hidden cost when adaptation becomes your primary leadership posture. When you're always adjusting, you're always scanning. When you're always scanning, you're always managing. And when you're always managing, you're not resting in the freedom of being one person.

This is the unspoken problem sitting beneath many leadership conversations. We talk about burnout, confidence, communication, boundaries, or balance. We recommend assessments, strategies, and skills. But many leaders aren't struggling because they lack tools. They're struggling because they're fragmented.

Fragmentation happens when identity, influence, and lived experience are required to shift independently of one another. It happens when leaders learn to survive and succeed by compartmentalizing who they are. It isn't a failure of character. It is a response to complexity, and it's especially common among high-capacity leaders who cross cultures, sectors, expectations, and systems.

Fragmentation is often rewarded before it is costly.

For a while, it can look like flexibility or emotional intelligence or even professionalism. Over time, an internal strain surfaces that no amount of performance can resolve. Leaders begin to feel tired in ways that don't match their workload because they sense inconsistency in their presence. They feel the quiet pressure of having to decide which version of themselves is required in each room.

The I^3 framework didn't begin as an intentional model. It emerged out of necessity. I needed a way to understand what I was seeing in myself and the leaders I served. I needed language that held complexity without diminishing it, and a framework capable of addressing leadership across systems, cultures, and callings without asking people to abandon parts of themselves in order to belong.

Identity. Influence. Integration. That is what I^3 represents.

Identity refers to who you are beneath roles, expectations, and performance. It is your core self and the part that remains stable when environments shift and titles change.

Influence refers to how your presence, voice, and authority are experienced across environments. It is leadership that flows from identity rather than performance for approval.

Integration refers to your capacity to live and lead as the same person everywhere. Being the same person everywhere means showing up authentically, without assimilation, without dimming your light, or without losing your identity.

You cannot skip one of those I-words and expect the others to hold. You can influence without identity, but it becomes performance. You can have a strong sense of identity without influence, but without influence, that clarity remains personal and rarely impacts your surrounding world. You can pursue integration without identity, but you will only assimilate with better language.

I^3 is the architecture that holds you through transition.

This book is organized in four parts, and each builds upon the previous part.

Part I: The problem names fragmented leadership and traces its roots. You will see how high-capacity leaders learn to survive through adaptation, how that adaptation becomes rewarded, and how its hidden costs accumulate over time. This section allows you to recognize the fragmentation in your own story before you can address it.

Part II: Identity focuses on strengthening your core. You will learn to distinguish between anchored identity and adapted identity, reclaim what performance has buried, and build a foundation that remains steady across environments. This is where the I^3 framework is fully introduced.

Part III: Influence shows you how to lead from who you are. You will learn how to clarify between identity and roles, understand what it means to lead from conviction rather than approval, and release your voice without performing for acceptance. This section develops concepts such as role compression, capacity of the room, and lethal loyalty.

Part IV: Integration equips you to thrive everywhere. You will learn the difference between code-switching and integration, how cultural intelligence meets anchored identity, and what it looks like to practice being the same person in every room you enter. This section moves from concept to lived posture.

Each chapter closes with a Quiet Declaration and a Reflection section with questions designed to move you from understanding into practice. This isn't a book to complete, but a book to live.

This book was written for leaders who are effective but unsettled, successful but fragmented, trusted by others yet unsure how to hold themselves together across the many places they are called to lead.

It is especially for female leaders, Christian women of African descent, and others who navigated spaces where their presence carried weight before they opened their mouths. It is for executives, founders, and pastors in major transitions. It is for globally mobile and multicultural leaders who learned to cross boundaries and now need to integrate what they carry.

If you've been told you are "too much" in one environment and "not enough" in another, this book is for you. If you sense that the next stage of leadership isn't about doing more but about becoming whole, this book is for you. If you have stood in a metaphorical bathroom, gripping the sink, wondering who you are beneath all the versions you created to survive, this book is for you.

This book is not about becoming a better version of yourself. It is about becoming integrated by living and leading as your authentic self.

The chapters that follow will not offer quick fixes. They offer language, reflection, and a framework for understanding the deeper work underneath the visible effort. This is an invitation for you to examine where fragmentation has been rewarded, where integration has been delayed, and what it might mean to lead from coherence rather than performance.

This is an invitation to anchor adaptability—not abandon it; to engage from a grounded center—not withdraw. This is an invitation to live as the same person everywhere instead of becoming someone new.

That is the journey ahead.

And it begins with a simple question that requires everything you have to answer honestly: Who are you when no one is grading you?

Turn the page and let us find out together.

PART I

THE PROBLEM — FRAGMENTED LEADERSHIP

CHAPTER 1
THE EXHAUSTION OF EVERYWHERE

The deepest fatigue is not physical.
It is the quiet erosion that happens when you keep editing yourself to belong.

~ **Alicia Partee**

I was 27 years old when someone thanked me for changing their mind about Black people. What was intended as a compliment landed like a weight.

There is an exhaustion that doesn't show itself as weakness or inability to perform, lead, or carry responsibility. It shows up in high-capacity leaders who continue to perform, produce, deliver, and hold systems together as they quietly carry the strain of having to be too many versions of themselves.

This exhaustion is not about workload. It is about weight—the weight of expectation, visibility, being measured by more than your work, and the weight of knowing that in certain rooms you are never only you.

You are also an idea, a representation, a test case, or a story that somebody wants to confirm. I learned this before I had language for it, and long before I developed the I^3 framework.

My career began with an unusual pattern. I was a forerunner, not in the romantic sense of taking risks for the thrill of it, but in the lived reality of being placed ahead of what my formal education or résumé should have guaranteed. Doors opened. Roles expanded. Responsibility arrived quickly. I kept up because that's what I was built to do.

There are people who enter organizations and need time to warm up, find confidence, and settle into their voice. That wasn't my story. I walked into spaces and could see what was missing. I could identify gaps, name what wasn't working, and propose a path forward. Though I was young, I was observant. I lacked years and experience, but I had discernment. I could read systems and people and move quickly and decisively towards results.

That kind of capacity gets rewarded, especially in high pressure environments and spaces that value outcome more than formation. It's called leadership. It's also called potential or talent, but it is rarely called costly, and an expense it is.

One of the first places that cost surfaced was when I served as a trainer at a Fortune 500 multilingual operations center. This wasn't a small operation. In fact, it was a high stakes corporate environment where language was the product, performance was measured across cultural and linguistic lines, and the standards I set rippled through teams I might never meet.

In that setting, language wasn't simply communication. It became identity, belonging, and power because whoever set the training standards also shaped the culture of performance. At some point, I was asked to train and lead a Cantonese-speaking team.

On paper, it was unconventional. I am not from a Cantonese-speaking country, nor did I share that cultural background. And yet, the leadership team trusted me because I had proven that I could produce results. I taught, organized, and translated complexity into a manner that people understood and followed. I motivated teams to execute results.

So, there I was. I had entered a culture that wasn't mine, carrying responsibility much bigger than my title, and did what I'd learned to do, I performed with excellence.

Six weeks into the assignment, I learned things about my team that no training manual could've prepared me for. For instance, I saw footprints on the toilet seats! That sight told me that some of my team members came from cultures where squatting was the norm; Western plumbing was foreign to them.

Management posted signs on how to use the facilities that ranged from 'do not stand on the toilet seats' to 'use seat covers to squat.' I remember looking at those signs and realizing this was something that went beyond restroom etiquette. These were first generation workers who were navigating a world with vastly different assumptions about everything, including how bodies are supposed to occupy space when relieving themselves.

We shared meals together. I remember the day they'd saved the eyes of a fish for me, presenting them as an honor because, in their culture, they were the best part of their meal. I didn't flinch but received the gesture for what it was, an offering. I didn't eat the fish eyes. I graciously declined and said we all deserve the best!

In return, I offered my own culinary invitation, cornbread dressing, when we gathered for a potluck. As I watched them taste the cornbread I'd made using my grandmother's recipe, a symbol of my cultural inheritance, I sensed a bridge forming between us. It wasn't about being the same or alike, but it was a bridge of mutual willingness.

What I taught this team was more than things related to work. For instance, the onboarding curriculum included a section on benefits education, and I took it seriously. I explained retirement savings in practical terms, using personal stories that I thought would stick, hoping they would understand that building a future was both possible and available to them right then and there, in a country that was still learning their names.

And then Amy said the thing.

It was an ordinary moment between two women as we stood in the training room while a session was wrapping up. She turned to me and said with what felt like genuine warmth, "You really changed my mind about Black people. I thought you were all lazy and didn't save money."

The words hung in the air. Time didn't stop, but something inside me went very still.

In the seconds before I responded, my mind moved through six weeks of shared meals, bathroom signs, fish eyes, and cornbread. I thought about the colleague who looked at my fair skin, then looked at my son's rich, beautiful brown complexion, and told me it was genetically impossible for him to be mine. I thought about all the times I had been a first encounter—the first Black woman, the first Black professional, the first Black anything—for someone who had only known my people through a story they'd heard somewhere. I thought about the weight of being a pioneer without ever having volunteered for the role.

And then I smiled and thanked her. I felt my face arrange itself into appreciation while something else happened underneath, a recognition of carrying someone else's assumptions the entire time, performing against a script I never wrote.

Amy didn't know what she had just revealed. She didn't realize she had shown me the architecture of belief she had been living inside. She didn't realize that for six weeks, while I was teaching her team, eating their honored dishes, and sharing my grandmother's recipes, she had been watching me through a frame that said, Let's see if this one is different.

She didn't realize she'd placed me in a category I'd never created, then handed me the burden of disproving it. She didn't realize she had turned me into an exception and called it a compliment. She didn't realize that the "mind" she claimed I changed was never just about me. It was about her story of who I was supposed to be.

That moment didn't offend me. It awakened me.

It showed me I was never just a trainer. I was a proxy, a reference point, and a living contradiction. It showed me that leadership, for some of us, comes with an additional assignment of being required to manage meaning, not only metrics. You are required to lead results and manage the room's assumptions, so that your presence doesn't threaten the order other people expect.

Looking back, I now carry something I didn't have in that training room. I am proud of how I impacted an entire team and their thoughts about an entire group of people. I am proud that my presence, competence, warmth, and willingness to receive fish eyes and offer cornbread became a living rebuttal to a lie they had inherited. I didn't ask for that assignment, but I completed it. And completion has a dignity of its own.

But pride doesn't erase cost. It accumulates in ways that show up later.

So, I adapted—not because I was false—because I was intelligent. I learned to be excellent and careful at the same time. I learned to carry myself in ways that reduced other people's discomfort. I learned to communicate in a way that landed. I learned to anticipate what would be misread, and I learned to preempt what would be projected.

This is where the seed of fragmentation begins—not in failure, but in success.

Except that isn't quite true because the seed was planted earlier. Much earlier.

I was born with nystagmus, a condition that affects how my eyes track and focus. At the time of my diagnosis, doctors didn't know much about it. They put me in glasses and sent me into the world as if I were a fully sighted child even though I wasn't. I couldn't see people across the street or recognize faces at a distance. The world beyond a certain radius was a blur of shapes and movement, and no one adjusted the expectations to match my reality.

So, I built my own systems.

My cousin and I developed a counting method. She'd tell me when someone was approaching, and together we'd count the steps until I should say hello. Three, two, one—now. I learned to time my greetings so no one would know I couldn't see them coming. I learned to recognize things and people before I could clearly see them. I learned that survival meant building invisible scaffolding around the gaps the world didn't make room for.

That was where the operating system got installed. It wasn't in a training room or boardroom. It began within a child's body that was told to function like the rest of society, even when functioning required inventing systems no one else needed.

And then it was reinforced when I was 16 as I became a mother. Two weeks after our baby was born, the father died. In the space of a month, I experienced birth and death, joy and grief, and a sudden reckoning with a future that looked nothing like I'd imagined. The world could have crushed me, but my family was there.

My grandfather, Johnny Ballard, was a quiet, steady man who worked as an upholsterer for the airlines. He also sewed my first cheerleading outfit and never spoke an ill word about anyone. He was there.

My mother, Patricia, was my protector and mama bear. She was there.

Together, they showed up in a powerful way, never lecturing or shaming but just holding me. It is because they held me that I was able to keep going. I went back to school, and I returned to work. I just kept moving

That was the second installation of the operating system. It wasn't adaptation. It was the belief that no matter what happens, I had to keep performing. I had to keep showing up—all the time, for everything. To stop showing up was never an option; nor was it ever modeled. The only option was to keep going and not stop. Period.

By the time I entered the workforce, adaptation wasn't a strategy. It was my first language. I didn't know there was supposed to be a stop button because I had never been given one. It was a lesson, and I want you to see how it was learned.

When you are a high-capacity leader, you develop skills that help you survive and advance. You become perceptive, socially intelligent, and a strategist with language and presence. You learn what each environment rewards, punishes, and how to move within that system without being crushed by it.

The world refers to this in several ways: emotional intelligence, professionalism, or polish.

The problem with any of those ways of showing up looking so polished, professional, and emotionally intelligent is there are hidden costs.

When adaptation becomes your primary leadership posture, it also means you're always adjusting and scanning. When you're always scanning, you're always managing, and when you're always managing, you're not resting in the freedom of being one person.

If you're nodding as you read this because you too have felt the weight of being watched while you work, or if you've edited yourself before entering a room, or smiled when you wanted to scream, or wondered why success still feels like a test—you are not alone. You aren't imagining things. The cumulative result of these costs is real, and it called "code-switching."

The complexity of code-switching is that it isn't inherently wrong, and it isn't inherently wrong because it is the reality for many people.

Code-switching is the practice of shifting language, tone, behavior, or presentation across different social and cultural environments. It is often wise, necessary, and it can be a useful tool. Someone asked me, "what is the difference between code switching and diplomacy?" Code-switching and diplomacy are closely related, as both involve the strategic, context-dependent adjustment of communication, behavior, and language to navigate different environments and manage relationships. While diplomacy is formally conducted between nations, code-switching operates as an interpersonal, daily, or professional form of 'micro-diplomacy.' Both are used to build rapport, ensure understanding, and manage perceptions in diverse settings. The issue is not whether someone code-switches. The issue is whether code-switching replaces identity, whether constant shifting becomes the only way you know how to belong, and whether leadership is reduced to performance instead of presence.

When I was at work, I knew how to show up, deliver, lead teams, train people, raise standards, and earn trust. I knew how to read the room and adapt the message. Those are real competencies that became useful tools in building my career.

However, at home, the same operating system followed me because I couldn't leave myself at the door. People say you should. Cultures imply you must. Families hope you will, but you can't—and I certainly couldn't. The self you bring to work isn't a separate self. It is still you. The question isn't whether you will bring it home. The question is whether you will know how to express it relationally rather than operationally.

My ex-husband told me I ran my home like a business. When I first heard that, it felt like criticism because I heard it as a statement that my strengths were out of place, and my way of thinking belonged in a boardroom, not in our marriage.

He wasn't entirely wrong even if neither of us understood what to do with it. Our home ran on a schedule. During the week, the rhythm was precise: breakfast, get ready for school, school, homework, sports, free time, bathe, and sleep. Rinse and repeat. There was no ambiguity. There was no drift. Everyone knew what came next because I'd designed it that way. If I'm honest, I was a little like a drill sergeant. Just a little.

Saturdays were cleaning days. When the music started, it was the signal. Everyone was supposed to be up out of bed, contributing to their assigned tasks. I rotated responsibilities and expected results. To this day, my middle son can clean a bathroom better than anyone I know. He learned excellence in that house. He also learned that when you commit to something, you do it thoroughly. Those are not small gifts.

But I look back now and wish I had been more affectionate. I threw the kids great parties. We spent time with family. Holidays were rich with people and food and celebration. But I was more like Martha than Mary in the Bible, working through instead of slowing down. Moving toward the next task instead of relishing the moment that was already here.

Years later, when my middle son was in his 30s—the one who climbed into bed to watch movies with me, the one I thought I was closest to—said, "You didn't provide the emotional support for me."

At first, I did not understand. I wanted to defend myself. But when I reflected, I saw it. I had been there. I had been present. I had scheduled and organized and provided. But I had not always stopped to *be*. I had not always sat without an agenda. I had not always asked how he was feeling and then waited, really waited, for the answer.

That is the collateral damage I carry. Not from malice. Not from carelessness. But from an operating system that I never learned to pause.

The missed opportunity was not that I was organized. It was not that I was decisive. It was not that I was a builder. The missed opportunity was that we did not know how to translate strength into intimacy. We did not know how to leverage leadership capacity with tenderness and partnership. We treated it as something to shut down, rather than something to integrate.

And that is the subtle tragedy of fragmentation. It teaches you that parts of you are acceptable only in certain places, and it teaches the people around you to treat your strengths as a threat instead of a gift that needs proper framing.

It also trains you to believe that success requires compartmentalization.

You learn to separate the parts of yourself, not because you want to be inauthentic, but because you want to be effective. You want peace. You want belonging. You want to be understood. So, you create versions. Not out of deception, but out of survival.

Then you get rewarded for it. Promotions. Recognition. Being the one who can fix the system. Being the one who can build something out of nothing.

After leaving my corporate role, I found my way to Silicon Valley during the dot-com era. It was a world of speed and promise, companies offering substantial salaries sweetened with stock options, everyone racing to build the next thing before someone else built it first. I thrived in that environment. Not because I loved chaos, but because I could see through it.

I was good at assessing an organization quickly, identifying what was broken, what was missing, what had never been built in the first place. I could create processes and procedures where none existed. I could write technical documentation that turned confusion into clarity. I could lead teams in fast-paced environments where the ground was always shifting.

The startup world let me be creative and innovative. It rewarded the part of me that could walk into a room full of uncertainty and start building. I became so effective at this that recruiters stopped coming for just me. They started making offers for my entire team. We were a package. A proven unit that could be transplanted into a new company and start producing results immediately.

We took one of those offers. The whole team. We moved together into a new organization because we had become something more than individuals, we had become a system that worked.

But here is what most leaders do not realize when they are being applauded for competence: if you do not integrate internally, your achievements become another layer of identity pressure.

You become the one who delivers. The one who produces. The one who exceeds expectations. The one who holds it all. The one who can manage complexity. The one who can navigate culture. The one who can make people comfortable. The one who can translate, bridge, and fix.

And you will keep doing it, because you can.

And you do it without stopping—until you start feeling the exhaustion that does not match your workload. The heaviness that does not match your calendar. The internal fatigue that comes from having to decide which version of you is required today.

This is what I mean by "the exhaustion of everywhere." It is the fatigue of carrying inconsistent expectations across multiple domains and trying to meet them all without losing your center. It is the fatigue of being praised for adaptability while quietly losing coherence. It is the fatigue of feeling that your leadership presence changes depending on the room, not because your values change, but because you have learned which parts of you can be seen safely.

What I grieve now is not the work. The work was real. The results were real. The impact was real.

What I grieve is that I did not have the knowledge then to balance. I did not know how to stop and feel. Each role came with its own objectives, its own goals, its own pressures, and I was programmed to perform. No matter how high the stakes, I was going to see it through to the end, and it was going to be better than what I found. That was the promise I made without ever speaking it aloud. That was the only way I knew how to be.

I wonder sometimes how much collateral damage I left behind. Not from malice. Not from carelessness. But from a system that had no stop button, running inside a woman who had never been taught she was allowed to pause.

My mother, Patricia, has told me my whole life: "You do too much." She has also told me I am brave because I was the only one in our family who got up and moved from California to Atlanta, Georgia, to places where no one knew me and I knew no one. She saw the drive. She celebrated the courage. But she also saw the cost—even when I could not.

Years later, I moved to Norway, a country where I could not understand every word being spoken and still felt foreign in my own skin. I finally had a name for what had started in that counting game with my cousin, for what had deepened in that Cantonese training room, for what had calcified in those Saturday morning cleaning sessions at home. The pattern followed me across oceans. Adaptation stopped working. And integration became unavoidable.

This is the reason so many high-capacity leaders misdiagnose their issues. They assume they need to work on confidence. Or communication.

Or boundaries. Or time management. Or another assessment. Another profile. Another label to explain themselves.

But the deeper issue is often more precise.

It is not a performance problem.

It is an integration problem.

Change is external. It is the job shift, the promotion, the relocation, the new team, the new environment, the new expectation. Transition is internal. Transition is what happens inside you as you move through change, the meaning you make, the identity shifts you absorb, the beliefs you inherit or reject, the roles you keep or release. You can move through change quickly and never transition well at all. And when transition is unfinished, fragmentation becomes the default coping strategy.

You become effective everywhere and internally divided.

This chapter is not designed to solve that yet. It is designed to name it accurately, because language is often the first form of freedom. Until a leader can name fragmentation, they will keep trying to repair it with performance. They will keep adding skills to a system that is already strained. They will keep trying to manage exhaustion with tactics, rather than addressing the deeper question of coherence.

The purpose of this chapter is to place a mirror in front of you, the reader and say: "If you have been feeling tired in ways you cannot explain, if your leadership presence feels inconsistent across environments, if you keep succeeding and still sense something unsettled inside, you are not behind, and you are not broken. You are likely carrying the cost of fragmentation.

And when you can name it, you can begin to address it."

But naming is only the beginning. There did come a day when I stood in a country where no one knew my credentials, where my résumé meant nothing, where the strategies that had carried me across every environment finally stopped working. And in that moment—as I stood in a dark bathroom, gripping the edge of a cold sink, staring at a reflection I no longer recognized—I answered the question I had been avoiding my whole life: "Who am I?"

A Quiet Declaration

Your exhaustion may not be a sign that you lack capacity. It may be a sign that you have been carrying too many versions of yourself across too many spaces, for too long, without a framework for integration.

Reflection

Consider these questions across all areas of your life, including work.

- Where have you learned to edit, soften, or relocate parts of yourself in order to be accepted, effective, or safe?
- What strengths have been labeled as "too much" in one environment, even though they were celebrated in another?
- What systems did you build in childhood that are still running today, and what would it mean to finally give yourself permission to pause?
- If you were no longer required to perform coherence, what would it look like to live it?

CHAPTER 2
WHEN WHO YOU ARE STOPS WORKING

The moment who you are stops working
is often the moment you finally start becoming who you are.

~ **ALICIA PARTEE**

When I moved to Norway in 2013, I believed I was prepared.

I had prepared in the way high-capacity leaders often do when facing transition. I researched relentlessly. I studied systems, structures, and schedules. I learned the geography of the place before my body ever touched the ground. I knew where the language classes would be held, when they would begin, the county we would live in, what stores were nearby, how transportation worked, what the weather demanded, and what clothing to wear that would allow me to move about without standing out too much.

Preparation had always been my way of entering the unknown. It had served me well across industries, across cultures, across leadership roles. I trusted preparation in the same way I trust a bridge I crossed hundreds of times. And when friends assured me that my life in Norway would be relatively easy, that I would learn the language, find work, and settle in, I believed them. Their confidence matched my own.

What I did not yet understand was that preparation can organize logistics, but it cannot protect identity.

We arrived in October. The air felt sharper than I expected. It seemed to be carrying something metallic and unfamiliar. The days were shorter than the calendar promised. Because Norwegian classes would not begin for a few months, I filled the waiting time with intention. I learned how to move through the city without fear, or at least, without showing it. I navigated my way on buses and trains, and I watched people for cues about how to stand, where to look, when to speak. I mapped my surroundings with the precision of someone who knows that competence can be performed even when confidence is thin. I refused to shrink inward. My husband, Dr. Tyrone Partee, walked beside me, steady and patient, his presence a quiet tether as I oriented myself to a place that was orderly, beautiful, and quietly foreign in ways I could not yet name.

I will always remember what Tyrone did for me in those first months. He'd lived in Norway for many years before we met. He was fluent in Norwegian. He understood at a deep level what I was going through. And he made sure I never felt dependent or diminished. He put money on a card for me, every week, without fanfare, without making me ask. Not once during our years in Norway did I feel like I did not have what I needed to go out, to enjoy myself, to live.

After a divorce earlier in my life, I had been the sole breadwinner for many years—a single parent who worked and provided and never stopped. Now I was in a country where I could not work, where I had to learn an unfamiliar language, where I could not contribute to the household in the ways I was used to. That might have broken something in my psyche, but Tyrone never let it happen.

He would drive an hour, sometimes an hour and a half, to Sweden just to buy the food I loved and the spices I wanted use for cooking—ingredients that made me feel like myself. He set money aside so I could fly home during the holidays, Thanksgiving and Christmas especially, because he knew those were the times I would be saddest to miss.

His actions were quiet. Steady. Not overly emotional. He gave me a place to rest. A space where I did not have to perform. And that was the foundation I stood on during the hardest years of my life.

When language classes finally began, I found myself seated in a classroom saying the ABCs and counting numbers aloud.

And then a familiar problem surfaced—the nystagmus. My eyes shake involuntarily. Glasses do not correct my vision; they address other issues like astigmatism, but the shaking remains. The world beyond a certain distance looks blurry to me, no matter what lenses I wear. And in that Norwegian classroom, sitting at an adult desk, while trying to learn a new language, I could not see the board.

Echoes from my past were immediate. Visceral. I was a child again. Sitting in a classroom with a last name (Williams, at the time) that placed me in the back row. I could not see the board then, either. But I had glasses on, so no one believed me. I remember throwing my glasses in front of a bus once, frustrated beyond words, saying "They don't help!" My mom was angry. My friends stared. And still, no one believed me. I realize now, they just did not understand.

So, I adapted. I put my head down on my desk and learned by listening. When tests were written on the board, I failed them. When they were handed to me on paper, I passed. My GPA suffered not because I lacked intelligence but because the system could not see what I could not see. Eventually, the school called my mother. They thought I was on drugs. But I was just a child with shaking eyes, wearing glasses that signaled normalcy while delivering none of it. My brother used to tease me by saying, "Your eyes are doing the Hustle." The Hustle was an old wall-to-wall dance. I still smile at that memory, not because it's funny, but because no one but my brother knew what to call it or how to navigate it.

But there I was, decades later, a grown woman in Norway, sitting in a language class with glasses on my face, unable to see the board. The instructor was writing vocabulary I could not read. I felt the familiar feeling of being visible and invisible at the same time.

How did I adapt? I had technology. I could take pictures of the board with my iPhone and enlarge them until the letters became legible. I built a system, just as I had built systems as a child, counting steps with my cousin so I would know when to say hello to people I could not yet see. The tools had changed. The adaptation had not.

I did not realize until much later how familiar all of this was. How the pattern from childhood had followed me across oceans. How I had spent my whole life building invisible scaffolding around gaps the world refused to accommodate.

There is a particular exposure that comes with learning a second language later in life. It is not simply the difficulty of grammar or pronunciation. It is the confrontation with how your intelligence is perceived by others, and more painfully, how you perceive yourself. For those who are articulate, educated, and accustomed to competence, sounding unformed can feel like erasure. You know who you are. You know what you carry, the meetings you've led, the teams you've built, the complexity you've navigated. And yet the words available to you do not yet hold the fullness of that reality.

I later learned that adult language acquisition is often difficult, not because of capacity, but because of self-awareness. Adults hear themselves sounding less precise. Less nuanced. Less intelligent than they know themselves to be. And for leaders who have built lives around clarity and authority, it can feel like a quiet dismantling. Every halting sentence becomes evidence of inadequacy. Every grammatical mistake feels like a confession.

If you have ever moved to a new country, a new company, a new community and felt the ground shift beneath you even though nothing about your competence had changed you know that feeling. We call it 'culture shock,' though that phrase does not capture the true weight of it. Culture shock is more than disorientation. It is the slow realization that the rules you spent your life learning no longer apply. It is the humbling experience of being a beginner again, in a body that remembers being an expert.

To complicate matters for me, most Norwegians I met spoke English fluently. Their generosity made daily life easier, but it also limited my opportunities to practice. The very accommodation meant to help me integrate often kept me suspended at the surface. I could survive.

But I could not yet belong.

I took work where I could. Often, because I was a foreigner learning the language, those opportunities were unpaid or minimally paid. Volunteer roles. Community spaces. I ended up at a preschool. I respected the work deeply. I admired the people who devoted themselves to children and service. And I did not resent starting there. I told myself it was temporary. Strategic. A way in.

I wanted to learn. I wanted to contribute. I wanted to belong.

Still, beneath the activity, something else was happening. Something I could not yet name.

At one point, a Norwegian friend looked at my LinkedIn profile and told me plainly that if I wanted a job in Norway, I would need to scale back the information I'd provided. In his words, my background looked "crazy." What was "crazy" on it? Corporate leadership. Pastor. Licensed marriage and family therapist. To the people in Norway, it did not signal range. It signaled confusion. It signaled someone who didn't know who they were. My friend told me that Norwegians decided what they would be when they were in high school and then they did it for the rest of their lives.

I remember thinking: "God, You're everywhere all the time. Why would I have to delete my accomplishments? Why can't I be all of this?"

I understood who I was. I did not understand why other people couldn't understand who I was.

So, I did what many leaders do when belonging feels threatened.

I edited myself.

I was sitting in our small apartment in Norway. It was daytime. I had on a sweater and comfortable pants as I tried to assimilate, tried to be Norwegian. My laptop was open in front of me. Tyrone was not home. He probably would have told me not to do it, but this was my journey, my attempt to find a way in.

I did not do the task I'd set out for myself quickly.

I sat there for a long time, trying to figure out what to delete and what to enhance. I was not working with the best parts of me. I was working with a vision from someone else, trying to become the version they could accept. And that was hard.

Line by line, I removed parts of my life.

Deleted: Licensed Marriage and Family Therapist.

Deleted: Three years of seminary.

Deleted: A master's degree.

Deleted: Three thousand supervised clinical hours.

Deleted: Two state licensing exams.

Deleted: Years spent sitting with people in their most vulnerable moments, holding space for grief, for healing, for the slow work of becoming whole.

All. Gone with a click. But there was more.

As a pastor, I had deleted the communities I had served. The sermons I had written. The spiritual weight I had carried. The calling I had answered. Erased. Because someone told me that being both corporate and clergy made me look confused.

As an organizational development consultant, the systems I had designed no longer appeared on my profile. The cultures I had shaped. The organizations I had walked into and rebuilt from the inside out.

Each deletion was a small death. Quiet. Administrative. Unremarkable to anyone watching. And yet, profoundly disorienting.

I was not lying. I was disappearing.

The edited profile that remained was clean. Corporate. Coherent. It told one story instead of many. And it felt like I was standing in a room where no one could see me fully, even though I was right there in front of them.

Imagine being a whole person and then suddenly, your digits are missing, something about you has to become invisible because it's been interpreted wrong. That was me. I felt shame. Shame that I was doing it, and shame for being so dynamic. I felt shame for being who I was.

Legibility came at a cost I had not anticipated.

And then, at a new point in my integration, I remember my first Thanksgiving in Norway. I'd cooked the traditional American meal for my Norwegian friends. I wanted to share something of myself, something from home. I made a full, familiar spread: roasted turkey, macaroni and cheese, cornbread, yams with sugar and marshmallows—and did everything my grandmother had taught me.

They hated it.

Well, not all of it. They liked the turkey. They tolerated the macaroni and cheese. But the cornbread confused them! They thought it was cake and asked why it was served with dinner instead of dessert. With a look of genuine bewilderment, someone asked, "Who puts sugar on yams?"

I did not cry in front of them. But later, alone, I wept. I told myself I would never cook another Thanksgiving dinner in Norway. And I meant it.

But Tyrone saw me. He saw the tears I tried to hide when I left America after each visit. How I missed the pumpkin spice lattes, the Yankee brand candles, and the abundance I'd taken for granted at home. He saw how Thanksgiving and Christmas were the hardest times for me to be away from home, how the smaller shops near our apartment in Eiksmark did not carry what I needed to feel like myself. He made sure I could go back home during the holidays. He set money aside for flights. He gave me that gift every year.

That is what love looks like when a person is in a transition. Not fixing. Providing.

Weeks passed. Then months. Applications were submitted. Silence returned. The strategies that had always worked for me—preparation, adaptation, performance—were no longer enough.

And then there was a morning I will never forget.

It was winter. Norway is not just cold at that time of year. The cold is a presence. Darkness arrives early. Light does not return until late morning, and even then, it feels tentative, as though the sun itself is uncertain about showing up. On that particular morning, cold seemed to live inside the walls of our apartment.

I woke up and tried to walk toward the bathroom. My feet felt like rocks, heavy, dragging across the floor. I could not lift them properly. Everything in me felt weighted down, as though gravity had increased overnight, and no one had told me.

The tiles were cold when I finally stepped onto them. My breath caught, shallow and uneven.

I had not deleted who I was. I had added the expectations of others. And that addition had become a burden that did not free me. It crushed me.

The bathroom was dark. I did not turn on the light immediately. I stood there in the dim, my posture slouched. I have never had good posture, but this was different. This was collapse. My eyes were wet, though the tears had not yet come. My breath was short, almost mechanical.

And then I looked in the mirror.

My eyes met the eyes in the mirror. And that is when the tears started streaming.

I did not recognize the woman looking back at me. Not because she looked older or tired, though she was both. She was someone else. Someone constructed from other people's expectations. Someone who had tried so hard to belong that she had edited herself into invisibility.

I gripped the edge of the sink. The porcelain was cold under my palms.

And I asked aloud, to no one and to God at the same time: "Who am I?"

Not what do I do. Not where do I belong. Not what am I supposed to accomplish here.

"Who am I?"

The question did not rise from despair. It rose from disorientation. The strategies that had always worked were no longer working. The version of myself that had carried me across systems and cultures no longer knew where to land. I was not failing in any measurable way. But I was unraveling.

And in that moment, I turned toward faith. Not a practiced faith. Not a polished prayer. I came in raw form.

God—my Papa Father—has always been my source. Not people. Not systems. Not the approval of others. Him. And in that dark bathroom, with my hands gripping the sink and my reflection staring back at me like a stranger, I went back to the only foundation that had never shifted.

"Gid, you did not bring me this far to leave me. Who am I supposed to be here? Not who was I before. Not who do they need me to be. Who am I now?"

It was not one scripture. It was everything I stood on, everything I knew about Him, how He had been with me throughout my entire life. The counting systems I built as a child to navigate a world I could not see clearly? He was there. The training room where Amy thanked me for changing her mind about Black people? He was there. The Saturday mornings with music playing and children cleaning and a marriage straining under the weight of unintegrated strength? He was there.

And He was here. In Norway. In the dark. In the mirror.

What followed was not resolution. It was reckoning.

Around this time, I was supporting foreign students at a middle school through after-school programming. Technically, I was being paid, though far below what my experience would have warranted. Still, I loved the work. These were students integrated into Norway, most of them refugees, some who had come through love and circumstance. They were navigating displacement, learning new systems while carrying old identities.

They reminded me of myself.

I remember their hunger to belong. Their exhaustion from performing, performing better in school, performing better in sports, performing whatever version of themselves this new country seemed to require. They needed a safe space where they could take off their cape of doing. They were trying to find their place too.

They reminded me that survival is not the same as belonging.

Eventually, I was asked to give my first presentation in Norwegian.

I practiced carefully. I rehearsed aloud in the shower, in the kitchen, while folding laundry. I prepared both linguistically and emotionally. Speaking publicly in a second language is a particular kind of exposure, especially for someone who had spent most of her life being articulate and precise. I knew I would make mistakes. I told myself that was acceptable; that growth requires humility.

The day of the presentation, I stood in front of the room. I spoke in Norwegian. My voice was steady, even if my grammar was not. I made it through. The foreign students and their parents were gracious. Encouraging. Their smiles were generous, and their applause felt genuine. They knew there was courage beneath my effort. They had also stood where I was now standing.

During the presentation, questions were asked. I understood them. That was not an issue. The issue was that I did not yet have subject-specific language. I could converse about daily life—things like groceries, transportation, and weather—but I could not yet respond with nuance in professional or technical domains. Anyone who has learned a second language understands this distinction. Conversational fluency and subject fluency develop on different timelines.

Still, I felt competent. I felt seen. I felt, for the first time in months, like maybe I was making progress.

And then....

The person whose opinion mattered most to me, the person who had given me the opportunity to be there at the podium, pulled me aside and told me, matter-of-factly, that I was not learning Norwegian fast enough.

The Norwegian word that comes to mind is *knust*. It means 'crushed.'

I felt it in my body first, before my mind could process the words. My shoulders dropped as though someone had placed weight on them. My stomach tightened into a knot. The room seemed to dim at the edges. The praise I had received just minutes earlier faded into something distant, indistinct, unreachable, like the muted voices of adults in a Charlie Brown cartoon. All I could hear, replaying in my head, was the judgment.

"You are not good enough. You are not progressing fast enough. You are failing."

I stood there, nodding. My face arranged itself into something that looked like understanding. But inside, everything was collapsing.

I confronted that person a year later, still hoping for context or care. Hoping she would soften her comments, explain better what she'd meant, or clarify that it was not as harsh as it had sounded.

Her response was simple: "That was just how I felt."

No apology. No recognition of impact. Just a statement of her perception, delivered as though perception alone was enough to make it true.

What she may not have realized, and what often goes unnamed in moments of transition, is that people in unfamiliar territory are doing so much more than just learning skills. They are learning themselves in new ways. And any show of insensitivity in those moments does not motivate growth. It fractures safety.

From that moment on, my body learned something my mind had not agreed to yet.

Whenever someone spoke Norwegian to me, my chest tightened before I could respond. My pulse quickened. My thoughts scattered like papers blown off a desk. I understood the words being said, but fear interrupted my ability to speak. My mouth would open and then close again. The words I wanted to say felt lodged somewhere between my brain and my throat, unreachable.

I began to associate language with evaluation. And evaluation with threat.

I stopped speaking.

Not consciously. Not as a decision. Instinctively.

I withdrew. I put up a shield. I told myself it was temporary, that I would speak again when I was ready, when I was better, when I could do it without the possibility of being found inadequate. But readiness kept moving further away, receding like the horizon.

This is how fragmentation takes hold. Not through failure, but through silence.

You tell yourself you are protecting yourself. And maybe you are. But protection, taken too far, becomes isolation. And isolation, over time, becomes erasure.

My husband noticed something in me during those months. He did not have words for it, and neither did I. A lot of what I was going through I could not share because no one had ever given me language for it. And when you do not have words, and when you think you are the only one, you stay silent.

But he saw me. And one day, he said, "If you aren't happy here, we can move home." I will always remember that moment. He did not try to fix things for me. He did not explain away my angst. He'd offered me an exit—not because he wanted me to take it. He offered it because he wanted me to know I had one.

I did not take that exit. Just knowing I could leave made staying feel like a choice rather than a sentence.

That is what love looks like in transition. Not solving. Witnessing.

Later...months later...when I was president of the Professional Women's Network in Norway, I participated in a mentoring program. During one session, I shared that story with my mentor. I told her what had happened. I told her how it had affected me. I told her, with careful language and measured tone, that I was still working through it.

She listened, her face neutral, patient. And then she said something that landed like cold water: "Get over it. Start over."

It felt like a slap.

I felt immediate resistance. A tightening in my chest. A desire to defend myself, to explain, to make her understand why this was not something I could simply "get over." The wound was real. The fear was real. The silence I had built around myself was real.

But beneath the resistance, something else surfaced.

Recognition.

I have a friend who was a diving instructor. He once told me about a student who had panicked underwater and was thrashing, spiraling, and burning through his oxygen supply. My friend had to hit him hard enough to knock him out so they both could surface, breathe, and live.

Like that diver, I realized that knock me out was what my mentor had. She hit me so I could live.

She did not dismiss my experience. She refused to let it define me. She reminded me that healing does not come from avoidance, and that integration requires re-entry. Not perfection. Not mastery. Courage.

In her own abrupt way she told me that I had given that moment too much power. That I had let one person's evaluation become the lens through which I saw myself. That I had built a life around a wound instead of letting it heal and ignoring the scar tissue.

And she was right.

So, I did what she said.

I went to Oslo University and started learning the language again at the basic level. Alphabet. Numbers. Foundations. I sat in a classroom with people half my age and relearned things I had known as a child. And this time, I let go of the need to sound intelligent. I embraced the necessity of sounding human.

I made mistakes. I mispronounced words. I confused verb tenses. I forgot vocabulary words when I was in mid-sentence and had to ask for help. And slowly, so slowly I almost didn't notice, fear loosened its grip.

I learned that fluency is not the absence of mistakes. It is the willingness to keep speaking despite them.

Today, I can carry on conversations in Norwegian. I understand and read more than I can speak. I am still learning. I will always be learning. But I am no longer afraid to speak. I am no longer measuring my worth by fluency alone.

What changed was not just language.

It was posture.

Imagine dimming a light in a dark room. You learn that you cannot fully dim light. If there is even a crack, light is going to come through. That is what I learned in Norway. I had tried to dim myself, to make myself smaller, more legible, less threatening to systems that could not hold my complexity. But light does not work that way. It finds the cracks. It insists on itself.

Norway itself was my mirror. It did not allow my fragmentation to continue unnoticed. It forced me to confront the limits of performance-based identity and to choose integration intentionally.

Change happens externally.

Transition happens internally.

Every transition asks the same question: "Who will you become here?"

Not, "Who were you before?" Not, "Who do they expect you to be."

"Who will you become?"

This chapter was about the moment when who you are stopped working, not because it was wrong, but because it was incomplete. It was about the space where adaptation gave way to formation, and where identity was either quietly diminished or reformed.

You are always becoming.

The question is whether you will do so intentionally.

I did not yet know that the framework I was building—the framework that was going to hold me through every transition after—was already forming in that dark bathroom. And I didn't have a name for it.

That name would come. And it would change everything.

A Quiet Declaration

When familiar strategies stop working, it is not always a signal to try harder. It may be an invitation to integrate more deeply.

Reflection

- Where have you gone quiet in order to protect yourself?
- What part of your voice have you withheld because it felt unsafe to practice?
- What childhood adaptations are still running in your adult life, and what would it mean to finally update your system?
- If you re-entered as a learner rather than a performer, what might become possible?

PART II

IDENTITY — STRENGTHEN YOUR CORE

CHAPTER 3

THE THREE I-WORDS: A FRAMEWORK FOR WHOLENESS

I^3 gives you language for what you have felt for years—
the work beneath the work.

~ **Alicia Partee**

By the time I had lived through enough transitions, I stopped believing that the problem was a lack of ability.

That may sound obvious, but many high-capacity leaders spend years trying to solve the wrong problem with the right discipline. They assume that if they can think more clearly, work harder, become more organized, or master yet another framework, they will finally feel steady. So, they add tools. They refine communication. They strengthen executive presence. They increase productivity. They attend leadership conferences, read the books, implement the strategies.

And still, the deeper strain remains.

Not because they are failing.

Because they are fragmented.

Fragmentation is not always dramatic. It does not announce itself with a crisis or a breakdown. Often it is quiet. It shows up in the small adjustments you make without thinking. The way you modulate your voice in certain rooms. The way you edit a sentence before you send it, less for clarity, more for safety. The way you laugh at jokes that you don't think are funny just because everyone else is laughing. The way you feel yourself shift, subtly, almost imperceptibly, when you move from one environment to another.

It is the constant scanning. The internal calculation. The questioning: "Who do they need me to be right now? What version of myself will land best here? What parts should I emphasize? What parts should I hide?"

It is the pressure to become legible, even when legibility costs you some coherence.

And over time, it becomes the internal labor of being high performing across multiple roles while slowly losing the feeling of being one person.

By "one person," I do not mean "rigid." I do not mean "culturally insensitive." I do not mean "refusing to adapt." I mean *coherent*. I mean *anchored*. I mean you can enter different environments without splitting yourself into versions just to survive them.

That is what this chapter is about—that is why a framework exists.

The framework emerged not because I admired a theory, but because I needed language for what I was seeing in myself and in others. I needed a lens I could actually live inside. A way of interpreting patterns across corporate leadership, church leadership, global mobility, and entrepreneurship without reducing the complexity into categories that felt too small for the truth.

I call it I^3 because of the three I-words: Identity, Influence, and Integration.

The I^3 framework does not define a personality type. It is not a temperament model. It is not a label that explains you and then leaves you exactly where you found yourself. It is a diagnostic and developmental lens for leaders who are navigating complexity, transition, and visibility—especially those who have learned to survive through adaptation and perform through fragmentation.

Most assessments tell you what you prefer. How you operate under stress. How you interact with others. They can be useful. Many leaders have taken them all: personality profiles, behavioral styles, motivators, strengths inventories, leadership assessments. I have taken them too and I found insight in some of them. But here is what I also noticed: assessments often describe tendencies without addressing coherence. They offer insight without integration. They give language without formation.

And that is why so many leaders can accurately describe themselves and still feel divided.

I^3 begins where most assessments end.

It asks a different question. Not, "What type of leader are you?" but, "Are you the same person in all the places where you lead?"

That question is not meant to shame you. It is meant to locate you. Until you can locate fragmentation, you will keep using skills to correct it.

But skill cannot replace coherence.

You have a map inside you. How do I know this? When I stood in that dark Norwegian bathroom and asked myself who I was, I did not receive an immediate answer. What I received was a direction. God led me through a process I eventually came to call "harmony," an internal excavation of spiritual gifts, heart, talents, abilities, personality, and experience. And not just adult experience, either. Childhood experience too. The earliest versions of who I was before the world asked me to edit myself.

What I discovered was that everything I needed to integrate the who of "Who am I?" was already inside me. It had always been there. I just had not taken account of it.

I remembered candy. Several kinds of candies of the brand Jolly Rancher. Apple Sticks. Cherry sticks. Watermelon sticks. And a lollipop called the Charms Blow Pop. When I was in elementary school, my friends and I figured out how to melt down the apple stick candies, wrap them around the Charms lollipops, then repackage and sell them.

Who does that?

There was no label for it then. No one called me an entrepreneur. I was just a kid with an idea and the audacity to execute it. But looking back, I see the pattern. I have always been someone who sees gaps and builds into them. Someone who creates systems where none exist. Someone who moves towards results before anyone hands me permission.

That is not a skill I developed in adulthood. That is who I was before I had language for it.

This is what I mean when I say the map is already inside you. There is a through-line in your life, a pattern that was present since before you had credentials. Integration is not about becoming someone new. It is about excavating who you have always been and bringing that person into every room you enter.

I did not fully understand this until I was 20 years old.

I was sitting in a doctor's office, the same kind of office I had visited every year of my childhood. New glasses. Same problem. The world still blurred beyond a certain distance. My eyes...still shaking. Nothing ever changed.

And that day, I finally asked the question directly: "Every year I come here and get new glasses, and they don't help me see. Why?"

The doctor looked at me and said, matter-of-factly: "I know. Your eyes can't be corrected."

I felt a childhood burden lift.

All those years. All those classrooms where I couldn't see the board. All those times I said, "These glasses don't help" and no one believed me. All those tests I'd failed, not because I lacked intelligence, but because the system measured me against a board I could not see. All those moments of putting my head on my desk just to learn in my own way. The teachers who called my mother. The shame. The silence. The scaffolding I'd built around a gap the world refused to name.

And now, finally, the doctor confirmed what I had known my whole life.

I asked, "Why didn't you tell my mother?"

He didn't give me a good answer other than that the doctors back then didn't have the knowledge. No fault to my mother—she was my mama bear, my protector. She made sure I had access to the best education, the best resources she could find. But no one had given her the truth, so she couldn't give it to me.

What I understand now is that I had been having to adapt—integrating—for my whole life, and doing so without knowing it. The counting system with my cousin was my first attempt at integration. Adapting to a world that could not see what I could not see, without losing the self that was doing the adapting.

I did it so well that most people never knew. I had a map, but others could not see the bumps in its roads.

Years later, I posted something on Facebook celebrating nystagmus awareness and talking about my low vision. A friend from elementary school responded: "I'm so sorry you're going through that."

I wanted to laugh. I wanted to cry. I had been "going through that" my entire life. But I had integrated so seamlessly that she never saw the scaffolding. She saw what she'd expected to see—a girl with glasses who functioned normally. She did not see the systems I had built just to survive.

People see what they want to see. People see through the lens of their own capacity. And if you integrate well enough, they will never know what you are navigating underneath. That is both the gift and the burden of high-capacity leadership.

I learned that lesson again, years later, in the corporate world. One of my best bosses at AT&T was a woman named Jennifer Truitt. She was the one who saw me leaning too close to my computer screen, squinting at text others could read easily. She did something no one else had done—she bought me a magnifying screen. She found a way to accommodate what she observed without making it a deficit.

Jennifer taught me something I still carry: "Don't worry about titles. Do what you love." She saw my innovation, my drive, my results. She was one of the people who nominated me for the Golden Globe Award, and won. I was presented with this prestigious award at a ceremony in New Jersey, AT&T headquarters at the time

To this day, she still reaches out to me. One of the messages she left for me on LinkedIn was, "You're just killing it." That is what it looks like when someone sees you clearly and believes in what they see.

Do you know why a framework for wholeness is necessary? It's because the world is not asking leaders to be excellent in one domain anymore. It is asking leaders to be fluent across domains.

A leader today is expected to manage complexity, lead diverse teams, navigate cultural dynamics, communicate with precision, and carry emotional weight without disintegrating. Many are leading across geographies, across generations, across belief systems, across political climates, across rapid technological change, and across organizational cultures that shift faster than people can process.

At the same time, leaders are also spouses, parents, adult children, mentors, board members, community leaders, faith leaders, and human beings with private lives that do not pause because the public's calendar is full.

This is why fragmentation is common.

The leaders are not necessarily unstable themselves, but the demands on them are layered, and the expectations others have for them are often contradictory. It is difficult to find balance. One environment rewards assertiveness. Another rewards humility. This environment demands directness. That environment demands restraint. Some environments expect a leader to code-switch. Others expect leaders to "just be yourself," while quietly punishing the version of themself that does not match its unspoken norms.

Over time, the leaders in any of those kinds of environments learn how to survive by splitting. One part of their self is here; another self is over there. The costs of fragmentation become most apparent when transition intensifies.

A leader can navigate many environments through performance. But a leader cannot sustain themself without a personal framework for integration.

That is the place from where the personal I^3 framework emerged. I^3 names what is required for sustainable leadership across complex environments—competence and coherence.

The I^3 framework is simple in structure but deep in application.

The I^3 Framework

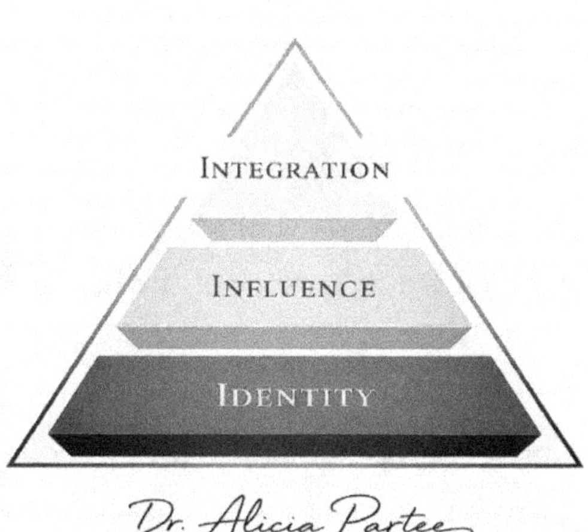

Each I-word has its own concepts, practices, and outcomes. Each I-word has its own form of strength. And each I-word answers a different question.

Identity answers: Who am I beneath roles, expectations, and cultural pressure?

Influence answers: How does my leadership presence land across environments, and what kind of authority am I operating from?

Integration answers: Can I show up as the same person everywhere, without assimilation, without dimming my light, and without identity loss?

You cannot skip one and expect the others to hold.

You can have influence without identity, but it becomes performance.

You can have identity without influence, but it becomes private clarity with limited impact.

You can pursue integration without identity, and you will end up assimilating again, just with better language.

The I³ framework is your personal architecture. It is meant to hold you through transition. And because it is architecture, it does not merely explain you. It supports you. It reveals structural stress. It points to what needs reinforcement.

Because the I³ framework was developed on top of my learned experience, you will further benefit from a deeper dive into its three parts.

Identity: Strengthen Who You Are

Identity is not your résumé. It is not your achievements. It is not your role. It is not your reputation. Identity is who you are beneath performance and beneath context.

I know what it feels like to confuse the two. When I deleted "pastor" from my LinkedIn profile, I was not just removing a job title. I was erasing my calling. I was silencing a part of myself that had answered something sacred. And when I stood in that dark bathroom and asked God and myself, "Who am I?" it was the moment I realized my identity had become tangled in roles I no longer held and environments that no longer recognized me.

Identity is what I lost in those deletions. And identity is what I found when I stopped asking what I should do and started seeking to find out who I actually was.

When identity is strengthened, a leader feels grounded rather than scattered. Clear rather than reactive. They are able to adapt without disappearing. They can change roles without losing themselves. They can receive feedback without collapse. They can be misunderstood without becoming unrecognizable to themselves.

Identity is what remains when the environment changes.

This is why transition reveals the question of identity so quickly. When you move from one world to another, the external cues that confirmed who you once were go away. The leader who was respected in one system feels invisible in another. The leader who had authority in one environment feels reduced in another.

When your identity is dependent on context, it will fracture under transition. Let me be clear: strengthened identity is not arrogance. It is not stubbornness. It is not self-centeredness. It is internal clarity, and it allows a leader to make decisions without constantly negotiating their worth.

Think of it this way: if you walked into a room where no one knew your titles, your credentials, your accomplishments, if you were simply unknown, would you still know who you are? Would you still feel like yourself?

That is the test.

Influence: Elevate How You Lead

Influence is not a title. It is not position. It is not volume. Influence is how your presence shapes environments. It is how your leadership lands. It is how trust is formed around you. It is the authority you carry, whether or not anyone names it.

I have walked into rooms I was not formally qualified to walk into and then watched doors open anyway. At one Fortune 500 company, their training program ran six weeks. I saw inefficiency. I put together a plan to cut it to four weeks without sacrificing quality. Leadership trusted me. They let me try. It worked. It saved money. Employees were still prepared.

No one gave me permission to see what I saw. No one handed me a credential that said I was allowed to redesign a system. But I had influence, the kind that comes not from title, but from presence. From clarity. From the willingness to name what others were stepping around.

Because God sets you up, I sometimes like to call Him "Jehovah Sneaky," a term I borrowed from longtime evangelist, Ed Silvoso. God places you in rooms before you are "qualified" and watches you discover that qualification was never the point. The point was alignment. The point was showing up as who you are and letting that shape the environment.

When I trained the team of Cantonese speakers at the Fortune 500 multilingual center, that was influence. My title did not confer influence but my presence did because I was willing to receive what they valued and offer to them what I carried. Influence was present because trust had formed in the spaces between us.

Influence that is elevated through I³ allows a leader to honor culture without surrendering identity. To adapt behavior without dimming essence. To learn norms without losing self.

Influence is not the absence of adjustment. It is the presence of coherence within adjustment.

Although influence itself is a neutral quality, it can be practiced two ways: with positive energy or with negative energy.

Here is what negative influence looks like: You walk into a room and you bulldoze over everyone and everything. You dominate. You make everyone feel uncomfortable. Because you secretly fear that you'll disappear, you perform a version of yourself that you may not recognize later. You've said out loud what you think needs to be said even though it is disruptive.

Here is what positive influence looks like in practice: You walk into a room. You notice the dynamics—who speaks, who defers, what is said and what is withheld. Then you adjust your tone, your pacing, your word choice. You honor the cultural norms present. You have no fear of being judged because you are leading with acceptance. This is presence without performance. This is influence with coherence.

Integration: Live as the Same Person Everywhere

Integration is the outcome most leaders long for but rarely know how to build.

Integration is not balance. It is not compartmentalization. It is not managing a calendar to make life feel calmer.

Integration is coherence across environments. It is the capacity to carry the same core self into each context, even when that context requires adaptation.

When I went back to Oslo University to learn how to understand the Norwegian alphabet, numbers, and other foundational words for living there, I stopped caring what people thought of me. The students were half my age. I joined their clubs. I sat in their language classes. I participated in everything. I let myself sound human instead of intelligent. I let myself be a learner instead of a performer. Had I mastered the Norwegian language? No. But I was learning to master integration. I had stopped fragmenting myself to meet expectations I'd never agreed to.

A side benefit happened when I discovered what I called the process of Harmony. God showed me that integration was not about becoming someone new. It was about excavating who I had always been and refusing to leave her at the door.

Your faith? Bring it with you.

Your personality? Bring it with you.

Your experiences—especially the childhood ones, the painful ones, the ones that shaped you before anyone handed you a credential? Bring them with you into integration and feel the Harmony.

Whatever you believe, wherever you go, it goes with you. That is integration. You need not apologize for who you are. Be unapologetic about what you carry.

Keep the Harmony in tune by knowing the difference between adaptation and assimilation.

Adaptation is learning the room.

Assimilation is losing yourself in order to be accepted in the room.

Authentic integration is adaptation without assimilation. It is showing up as the same person everywhere, not by refusing cultural awareness, but by refusing identity loss. It is refusing to dim your light for the comfort of others. It is refusing to fracture into other versions of yourself just to survive.

So, Identity, Influence, and Integration form a triangle where all three sides are of equal importance and create the three-part harmony necessary to be your authentic self in any environment.

I remain grateful for the way the I³ framework emerged in the way I noticed patterns across environments that should have felt unrelated. Corporate leadership has its culture, its language, its norms, and its metrics. I had lived in it for years. I understood it. I knew how to lead in that world, and I knew what belonging to it looked and felt like.

Then I transitioned into church leadership, and I found myself in an environment that felt like an entirely different culture. The expectations there were not written, but they were real. The language was different. The social norms were different. The criteria for being "accepted" were different. I was used to environments where competence and outcomes were celebrated. In the church culture, I sometimes felt evaluated by a different standard entirely. Not always explicitly, but in ways that were felt.

I'd had a mentor once, a pastor who was a spiritual father to me, a person who told me I was not "spiritual enough." I still do not know what being "spiritual enough" looks like, because I absolutely love God. I love His Word. I went to seminary not to become a pastor, but because I wanted to learn how to study the Bible. The doors to pastoral leadership opened after that, and I walked through them because I sensed a calling. But even then, my corporate background seemed to make some people uncomfortable. My confidence was interpreted as worldly. My professionalism was read as a lack of spirituality.

I did not want to fight. I wanted to belong. So, I did what many people do when entering a new culture. I assimilated. I joined the choir. I cannot sing well.

Looking back, it almost makes me laugh. I grew up Catholic. I attended Catholic school and went to mass. I do not remember a choir; just liturgical books and hymns sung by parishioners from the pews.

But when I moved to Atlanta in 1989, I walked into Wings of Faith Baptist Church. It was a huge, vibrant congregation with upbeat music and a choir that was really, really good.

Everything changed.

I remember my first Sunday there. The energy was unlike anything I had experienced. The pastor was singing, and in the song, he kept repeating a phrase from Jeremiah about the word of God being like fire "...shut up in my bones." He sang it over and over: "Shut up, shut up, shut up!"

I called my mother afterward, confused. "Mom, the pastor kept singing "...shut up, shut up, shut up. I don't understand. Does he want us to shut up?"

My mother laughed so hard. She explained the scripture, the context, the tradition. And I realized I had entered new ground I would have to learn to navigate it. The Old Testament. The stories of David. Jeremiah's fire. It was all new, all exciting, and it opened something inside me.

The choir seemed like a gateway into belonging. A friend invited me, and I thought, "Get in where you fit in. Surely, I can accomplish this." I did not audition. I just showed up. And I loved the dancing—we had movements in the choir, and dancing had always been easy for me. I had been a cheerleader in elementary school. I danced at the Girls' Club after school. My shaking eyes had nothing to do with dancing. I could move my body. I could feel the rhythm. That part of me was fully alive in that choir.

At first, no one noticed that I could not sing. There were so many voices. I blended in, or so I thought. But then came the day we were rehearsing for something significant. We were preparing to back up a major gospel artist, John P. Kee or Shirley Caesar, someone like that. The stakes were higher. The sound had to be tighter.

And the pastor, who was also the choir director, Pastor Dreyfus Smith, kept giving me the eye. At first, I thought it was a good sign. My old self assumed he was noticing my effort. Maybe I was doing well. Maybe a solo was coming.

Then I realized the truth. He was giving me the eye because I was off-key.

My mother and my husband had told me that I cannot hold a tune. I never fully accepted it. I still sing to this day. But that moment in rehearsal, when I realized the look was not praise but correction, something shifted.

I had joined something I had no business joining, just to belong.

I did not leave the choir immediately. I stayed for a while, trying to make it work. But eventually, I found my way to where my actual gifts could serve, administration, training, teaching, project leadership. I found the places where I could be myself and be useful. Places where belonging did not require performance I could not sustain.

That is the pattern of how people enter new environments and instinctively search for belonging. Then they can take roles that secure access. They soften their edges. They hide what might be misread. They become legible.

Do not call it fragmentation. Call it wisdom.

But here is what I learned: being in different roles does not require being a different person. The question is not whether you adapt. The question is whether you disappear while adapting.

This book does not ask you to become someone else. It does not ask you to optimize yourself into exhaustion. It does not treat leadership as a series of isolated skills to be mastered and stacked.

It invites you into coherence.

It helps you strengthen identity beneath roles and expectations.

It helps you elevate influence through presence rather than performance.

It helps you practice integration until "same person everywhere" goes from being a slogan to a lived reality.

This is not fast work. But it is lasting work.

And for leaders who have lived fragmented long enough, lasting is the point.

The chapters ahead will take each I-word even deeper. You will see how identity is strengthened. You will learn how influence is elevated. You will practice integration until it becomes embodied.

But before we go further, I want you to sit with some questions: What are you afraid will happen if you stop fragmenting? Are you afraid you will be rejected? Are you afraid that you will be too much? Are you afraid that the rooms you've entered will ask you to exit? Are you afraid that the rooms you want to enter will close their doors? Are you afraid that the people who accepted the edited version of you will not accept the whole version of you?

Name your fear. Until you name it, it will keep running you.

And then ask: "If you stop splitting yourself to survive, what would you have to believe about who you are?"

Not who you perform as. Not who they need you to be. Who you are. That is the work of I^3. However, knowing the framework is not the same as living it.

A Quiet Declaration

If you feel tired in ways that do not match your workload, it may not be because you need to do less. It may be because you are ready to become whole.

Reflection

- Where have you confused adaptation with assimilation?
- What environments reward versions of you that are not fully you?
- What map has been inside you since childhood, and what would happen if you finally let it guide you?
- If you practiced being the same person everywhere, what would have to change first: your environment, or your agreement with fragmentation?

CHAPTER 4
RECLAIMING YOUR CORE

Your core existed before the room started grading you.

~ **ALICIA PARTEE**

There is a version of leadership that looks admirable on the outside and feels expensive on the inside. It is the kind of leadership that learns early how to succeed, how to comply with expectations, how to deliver outcomes, how to earn approval, and how to survive systems that reward performance more than personhood. It is the kind of leadership that becomes disciplined, strategic, and productive, not because the leader loves excellence, but because the cost of failure feels too high.

For many high-capacity leaders, identity does not begin as something they define. It begins as something they learn to protect. And protection often looks like performance.

That is why the first movement of the I^3 framework begins with Identity. It's not because identity is trendy, nor because self-awareness is new. It is because without a strengthened core of identity, leadership is just an ongoing negotiation with the environment. You can be brilliant and still be brittle. You can be accomplished and still be uncertain. You can lead people and systems and still not know what is anchoring you beneath the role.

Identity is the core self that lies beneath roles, outcomes, expectations, and cultural pressure. It is what remains when the titles shift. It is what is stable when the environment changes. It is the part of you that should not need constant proof to be trusted.

Reclaiming your core is not about becoming someone new. It is about returning to what was always there, beneath what you learned to do to be safe, accepted, and rewarded.

There is a difference between anchored identity and adapted identity.

Anchored identity is stable enough to withstand feedback, transition, and cultural change without collapse. It does not mean the leader never struggles. It means the leader's sense of self is not dependent on constant external confirmation.

Adapted identity is not fake. It is formed through survival. It is shaped by the environments that rewarded certain behaviors and punished others. It learns quickly what will earn safety and what will invite rejection. It becomes skilled at adjusting to expectations, even when those expectations are unspoken. Over time, it can feel like the leader is successful everywhere yet feel unclear within themself.

Fragmentation often begins when adaptation becomes the primary way the leader learns to belong.

The system you learned taught you how to be. The I^3 system teaches you who to be.

When I look back, I can see how early my identity organized itself around performance. Was I shallow? No. I was young, observant, and trying to succeed inside systems that were clear about consequences.

I was around 20 years old when I started working at AT&T in a call center. The rules were strict. If you were late three times or absent three times, you could be fired. That kind of environment trains you quickly. It emphasizes discipline and teaches threat-based compliance. It teaches you that your stability depends on your performance, and that you are only as safe as your record.

So, I became disciplined. Perfect attendance. No lateness. No absence. I learned to show up no matter what. Even when I was sick. Even when my body was not well. I came in early. I planned for traffic. I mapped things out to the letter because I did not want to lose my job. I watched other people get fired—they were the young people, most of them between the ages of 18 and 21. They were just starting out. I knew I did not want to be fired.

But what I did not understand at the time was that the discipline I was developing was also shaping my identity. It was forming a belief that showing up perfectly was not simply admirable. It was necessary for survival.

And then there was the mirror. AT&T put mirrors on our desks. We were expected to smile while we talked, even though the customers could not see us. The logic was that a smile could be heard in your voice. So, I smiled. I performed a face for people who would never see it. I opened every call the same way: "Thank you for calling AT&T. My goal is to provide you with excellent service. How can I help you today?"

The fact that I still remember those exact words tells you how deeply the script was installed.

I was adapting to an environment designed to shape me into what the customer needed to experience. I was becoming what someone else required me to be. And I was good at it. My talk times were efficient. My quality scores were high. I did not get in trouble. I received good appraisals.

And when you are measured constantly, you begin to internalize measurement as worth.

You start equating "being good" with "being scored well." You begin to organize your sense of self around performance outcomes because performance outcomes are what the system recognizes. You may not say it out loud, but you begin to believe your internal dialogue: "If I perform well, I am safe. If I perform well, I belong. If I perform well, I am valuable."

The measurement did not stop when I advanced. It evolved.

As I moved into leadership, I became a quality assurance manager. Now I was the one listening to calls, scoring performance, and reinforcing standards. I was still living in a world where everything was evaluated, structured, quantified, and tied to outcomes.

So, when I became a manager over a team, I did what the system had trained me to do—

I focused on performance. I cared about numbers. I cared about results. I cared about execution. And I enforced the rules the way the rules had been enforced on me.

If someone was going to be tardy three times, or late twice and absent once, they were going to get fired. I did not care what happened. Life happens, but that was not my concern. The rules were the rules.

I am not like that today. Life happens, and I understand the need to be flexible. But back then, I had become the system. I was enforcing what had been enforced on me, and I did not yet see the cost.

One season, I was working two jobs. I was so exhausted that one day I showed up to one job wearing the uniform of the other. That is what performance-based identity costs. It does not announce itself as unsustainable. It just keeps demanding more until your body starts making the mistakes your mind refuses to acknowledge.

The messages you receive are what shape your behavior. For me, this pattern did not start when I moved into a corporate job. It started earlier.

My grandfather, Johnny Ballard, bought me a car when I was about 18 or 19 years old. He was proud of me, not necessarily because school was my strongest domain, but because he saw I was trying. I was working. I was pushing forward. I was becoming.

The car was a Hyundai. I could have chosen any car I wanted, but I picked that one because the graphics were just coming out, the kind that showed the door opening and closing on a screen. It felt modern. It felt like arrival.

There was just one problem: it was a stick shift, and I did not know how to drive one.

My grandfather drove it off the lot. Over the next few days, he tried to teach me. I scared him half to death. Eventually, my cousin took over and finished the job.

Here is the part that catches my breath now: I had not yet learned that my eyes could not be corrected. I was driving with shaking eyes, unable to fully see, performing as if I were normal because I did not even believe myself anymore. The world had told me so many times that I was fine with glasses on—problem solved—that I had stopped trusting my own experience.

When I think about the risks I took in those years, driving and working and navigating a world I could not fully see, I understand only now how deeply the performance instinct was already installed. I was not going to let anything slow me down. Not my body. Not my vision. Not my exhaustion.

I remember when my cousin said to my grandfather, "You got her a car and she's younger than me. Why did you not get one for me?"

"Because she works hard."

It was a generous and loving response. But it also carried a message that lodged itself deep inside me. Performance is what makes you worthy of provision. Performance is what makes you lovable. Performance is what makes you valuable.

Many leaders have some version of this story. Maybe not a car. Maybe it was praise. Maybe attention. Maybe approval. Maybe relief from criticism. Over time, the leader internalizes the idea that achievement is the pathway to security. And then the leader grows up.

The problem is not that achievement is bad. The problem is when achievement becomes identity. When achievement is your identity, you cannot rest. You cannot fail. You cannot be unknown. You cannot be ordinary. You must keep producing evidence that you are enough.

And evidence is never permanent.

So what happens when the system rewards your performance? I can say that the system shaped me and then it rewarded me. At AT&T, I received an award, a prestigious recognition that came with a trip to New Jersey, a ceremony, photographs, money, and a trophy. It was a big deal. I had earned it through innovation, through results, through being the person who could see gaps and build solutions.

It felt good. I will not pretend it did not.

But looking back, I can see how rewards strengthen the wrong foundation. Every award becomes reinforcement. Every recognition becomes proof. The message is clear—keep going. Keep achieving. Keep moving. The results are the results, and nothing else matters.

Did it feel hollow? Not then. Not in the moment of receiving an award. But there was something I could not bridge. I was thriving in business, but I did not know how to translate that into my social life, my family life, my interior life. The success had no translation. It stayed in its lane, impressive and yet isolated.

And when identity is built on what you do, every setback becomes personal. Every transition becomes destabilizing. The scaffolding holding up your sense of self is external, and external scaffolding can be removed.

There ia a cost when you over-identify with your performance in the perform-and reward system. What I did not yet understand was that performance is never the whole story. People are not numbers. Teams are not machines. Leadership is not simply about output. It is also about the internal world of the people producing the output and how they carry pressure, how they interpret expectations, how they experience being led.

I learned that the hard way.

While I was in seminary, I chose to lead a church-wide campaign, a 40-day initiative that would introduce small groups for the first time, QUESTION: What do you mean by "introduce small groups for the first time?" increase engagement, and deepen community. It was ambitious. It was exactly the kind of project I thrived on. I gathered a team and got to work.

The campaign was successful. We saw an increase in financial giving. We saw growth in church membership. People participated in small groups for the first time. By every measurable outcome, we had delivered.

But I also created some collateral damage on that path to success.

There was a woman on my team who was the exact opposite of my personality. She was detailed, methodical, and worked at a much slower pace. She asked a million questions. She wanted workflows and processes and time to think things through. She drove me crazy. I am sure I drove her crazy too.

My usual need to move forward, to see results, to keep momentum clashed with her need for thoroughness. And instead of learning how to bridge that gap, I made decisions without the team. I moved forward without them. Yes, we got results. But when I look back, they probably felt unseen. Unappreciated. Maybe even used.

I'd burned people out. And many people did not want to work with me on projects after that.

That is the trap of over-identification with performance. You do not simply pursue excellence. You become dependent on it. And when you are dependent on results, you will sacrifice relationships to get them, sometimes without even realizing what you are doing.

There is a story I hesitate to tell, but it captures this season perfectly. I was directing an Easter play at the church, a production called "The Rolling Stone." I poured myself into it. Rehearsals were scheduled. Deadlines were tight. And the actor playing Jesus kept showing up late.

One day, he was caught in traffic again. It was going to be his third time being late.

And I was going to fire him.

Yes. I was going to fire Jesus.

A friend at church pulled me aside and said, "You cannot fire Jesus. He's in traffic."

I had become so rule-bound, so performance-driven, that I was ready to fire the person playing the Savior in an Easter production because he'd violated the attendance policy I had internalized decades earlier at AT&T.

That is what happens when identity is built on performance. The system you survived becomes the system you enforce. And you do not always see the absurdity until someone names it.

Identity shaped by survival is often exceptionally competent. It learns quickly. It adapts. It performs. It finds the rules, even when they are unspoken. But survival identity is rarely free. It carries an internal pressure to keep proving. It carries the fear of being exposed. It carries a sensitivity to criticism that feels like threat.

This is why leaders can be highly accomplished and still feel internally unstable when they are in a time of transition. When the environment changes, the rules change. And if your identity is dependent on the rules, you will experience disorientation.

When I transitioned from corporate and startup work into church leadership, I expected the adjustment to be manageable. I was secure in what I could do. But not everyone was glad to see me. I'd become the first female pastor hired on staff at that church. People had opinions:

"Why her?"

"She's so unorthodox."

"What good can come out of Oakland?"

At first, I thought "unorthodox" was an insult. But maybe God chose me precisely because I was unorthodox. If I look back at my life, the patterns, the doors that opened before I was qualified, the rooms I entered before I had credentials, it was always me being who I was that took me where I needed to go.

But in that season, I did not have that clarity. I felt called and secure in my gifts, but with my spiritually I felt inferior. I wanted to be "spiritual enough." I wanted God to love me. I wanted to belong in a world that seemed to have rules I could not decode.

And I was misinterpreted. People thought I did not care because I did not show care the way they expected me to do. But I did care—I cared deeply. I just did not know how to bridge the gap between who I was and who they needed me to be.

Neither side knew how to connect. We were navigating murky water, and I felt that I did not have a map.

Years later, after living abroad for eight years, I experienced another kind of transition: coming home. We moved back to the United States from Norway in 2021. The reverse culture shock was worse than the original culture shock.

I remember walking into a grocery store in America and crying. There were hundreds of cereals to choose from. In Norway, there had been maybe four. The abundance was overwhelming. The choices were paralyzing. I stood in the aisle and wept, not because I was sad, but because I did not know how to be home anymore.

Your friends at home expect you to be who you were. But you are not who you were. You do not fit in the international community because you are home now. But you do not fit at home because your mind changed when you were in the international community. Your perspective shifted. You are internationally minded in a place that remembers you as local.

"Here I go again," I thought. "Another transition. Another environment that does not quite hold the fullness of who I have become."

That is what happens when your identity is not anchored. Every transition exposes the fractures. Every new environment becomes a test of whether you belong.

How can you put an anchor down, beneath your adaptation?

Reclaiming your core is not about rejecting your strengths. It is about relocating the foundation. For me, that foundation is God. He is my source. Anytime I have a question about identity, I go to Him. Not to people. Not to systems. Not to the approval of environments that cannot hold my complexity. I go only to Him.

I am who God says I am. Nothing about me needs to be erased. I am fearfully and wonderfully made. He knows the number of hairs on my head. He has bottled every tear. I am the apple of His eye. His plans are to prosper me, not to harm me.

That is not soft theology. That is anchored identity.

When I stood in that dark Norwegian bathroom and asked, "Who am I?" I went back to my source. I went back to the One who made me and called me and equipped me before any system handed me a credential. And from that place, from that anchored core, performance became an expression of who I was, not the proof that I was enough.

What about you?

You are not safe because you perform well. You are not valuable because you deliver outcomes. You are not lovable because you meet expectations. You are safe, valuable, and lovable because you are.

I am still learning this. I want you to know that.

Not long ago, my husband asked, "Can we have a week without talking about goals and objectives?"

I laughed. And then I paused. He was not joking. He was mirroring something back to me that I still had not fully integrated. The drill sergeant in me is quieter now, but she is not gone. She still shows up when someone I love is sick! I once drove Tyrone nearly two hours to a hospital because I decided he needed to go to the best emergency room, no discussion. He later told me I was not being sensitive. I was being functional. I was solving instead of feeling.

He was right.

Integration is not a destination. It is a practice. And I am still practicing.

What I have learned is that when identity is anchored, feedback becomes information, not indictment. You can hear critique without hearing rejection. You can receive input without defending your worth. Transition becomes formation, not threat. You can enter new environments without losing yourself. You can adapt without assimilating. Rest becomes possible. You are not constantly proving. You are not constantly performing. You can be still without feeling like you are falling behind. Failure becomes instructive, not identity-defining. You can make mistakes without believing you are a mistake. Leadership becomes generative, not extractive. You are not leading from depletion. You are leading from fullness. You have something to give because you are not constantly trying to earn your existence.

This is what I mean by reclaiming your core.

It is not about becoming someone new. It is about returning to who you were before you learned that performance was the price of belonging.

There is a strength that comes from proving yourself. And there is a strength that comes from knowing yourself.

The first kind of strength is impressive. It builds résumés. It earns recognition. It opens doors.

But the second kind of strength is sustainable. It withstands transition. It holds coherence under pressure. It does not fracture when the environment shifts.

This chapter is not about rejecting the first kind of strength. It is about integrating it into the second. It is about learning to be excellent and anchored. Disciplined and free. High-performing and whole. Because that is the work of identity; not self-improvement. It is self-reclamation.

Identity is the foundation. But it is not enough on its own because a leader can know who they are and still not know how to carry that into a room. That is where influence begins.

A Quiet Declaration

You were not created to be measured into worth. You were created to be anchored, so that what you produce flows from who you are, not the other way around.

Reflection

- Where did you first learn that performance equals safety?
- What parts of you became exaggerated because they were rewarded?
- What parts of you became hidden because they were misunderstood?
- If you no longer needed achievement to prove you are enough, what would become possible in your leadership?
- What would it mean to go back to your source and let that be the foundation you stand on?

PART III

INFLUENCE — LEAD FROM WHO YOU ARE

CHAPTER 5
IDENTITY VS. ROLES

Roles are meant to express identity.
The moment they replace it, you start disappearing in plain sight.

~ ALICIA PARTEE

Four years after I left Norway, a client reached out to me. We had worked together during her own international transition because she was a high-capacity leader who'd moved to a new country, struggled to find balance between motherhood, board leadership, and corporate responsibility, and eventually found her footing through the I^3 framework. When we finished our work together, she was grounded. Clear. Integrated.

And now she was back.

She had not regressed but her life had changed again. She had a new role, a new supervisor whose cultural background and leadership style were radically different from what she was used to, and she found herself slipping back into some old patterns of performing instead of leading, adapting instead of expressing, losing coherence in an attempt to belong.

"I thought I had this figured out," she said, "but I feel like I'm starting over."

She was not starting over. She was discovering what every leader eventually learns: integration is not a destination. It is a practice. The foundation we'd built for her together was still intact. She still knew who she was, but having entered a new environment with new demands, her roles were trying to recruit her back into fragmentation.

This is why Chapter 5 was written.

Chapters 1 through 4 established identity as the foundation of leadership coherence. You named fragmentation. You traced its origins. You learned to reclaim your core. But identity, once strengthened, does not exist in a vacuum. It expresses itself through roles. And those roles, if left unexamined, will work to replace what they were only meant to express.

This chapter is about dismantling the confusion between who you are and what you do because there is a difference between your identity and the roles you play.

Identity is the core self that remains stable across environments.

Roles are the containers through which identity is expressed.

This distinction sounds simple. It is not.

Most leaders intellectually understand that they are more than their job title. But understanding it is not the same as living it. When the role expands, when the role is praised, when the role becomes the primary way others recognize you, the boundary between identity and role begins to blur. You stop expressing yourself through the role. You start defining yourself by it.

This is where role compression begins.

Role compression is the gradual collapse of identity into function. It happens when leaders invest so much of themselves into what they do that they lose access to who they are beneath the doing. The role demands. The role expands. The role consumes. And because the leader is high capacity, they keep delivering until one day they realize they cannot remember what they wanted before the role told them what to want.

Role compression is not burnout. Burnout is about capacity depletion. Role compression is about identity erosion. You can be fully energized and still be role-compressed. You can love your work and still be losing yourself inside it.

The I³ Leadership Integration Assessment includes a statement that often surfaces the role compression pattern: "I know where my identity ends and my responsibilities begin." Leaders who score low on this item are not lacking discipline or clarity about their tasks. They are lacking separation between self and function. They have become so fused to their roles that any threat to the role feels like a threat to them.

Role compression rarely announces itself. It accumulates quietly, often disguised as commitment, excellence, or sacrifice.

Here are the role compression patterns I see most often in high-capacity leaders:

Decision fatigue that does not match your calendar. You have capacity. You have time. But you cannot decide what you want for dinner, what you want to do on a Saturday, what you want for yourself. The role has been making so many demands that your own desires have gone offline.

Excellence with an edge of resentment. You are still delivering. You are still exceeding expectations. But there is a quiet bitterness underneath it; a sense that you are giving more than you are receiving, that the role is taking more than it is giving back.

Grief you cannot explain. Nothing is technically wrong. The role is working. People are pleased. But you feel a low-grade sadness, a sense of loss you cannot locate. What you are grieving is yourself; the parts of you that have been compressed to fit the container.

Identity confusion during transition. When your role changes through promotion, demotion, relocation, retirement, or reassignment, you do not just feel disoriented. You feel erased. If the role was your identity, losing the role means losing yourself.

The Assessment also states: "I feel pressure to redefine myself to be accepted." Leaders who score high on this item are often caught in a cycle of role-based belonging. They believe they must become what the environment rewards in order to stay included. They are not adapting. They are assimilating. And assimilation, as we established in Chapter 3, always extracts a cost.

I experienced role compression as a lesson before I even knew what it was during my years in Norway. After the season of language learning, after the bathroom mirror moment, after I returned to Oslo University, I eventually found work at the United States Embassy. I became the general manager of a small store that sold American products to diplomats, military personnel, and local staff.

On paper, it was a step down. I had led training programs, built systems, pastored churches, navigated Fortune 500 complexity. And now I was managing inventory and revenue for a retail operation inside an embassy.

But I loved it.

The work was clean. Black and white. Bottom line. Either we were profitable under my watch or we were not. There was clarity in that. There was dignity in that. I was not performing for anyone's approval. I was simply doing the work.

And yet, it was role compression. That role used only a fraction of what I carried. My gift for teaching, and my skills in organizational development and leadership formation had no outlet. I was functional. I was not fully expressed.

Here is what I learned: compression is not always a crisis. Sometimes it is a classroom. That season at the embassy expanded me in ways the role itself could not contain. I interacted daily with diplomats, military leaders, and international staff. I learned to navigate protocol. I observed how power moves in institutional spaces. I saw how people with vastly different backgrounds and belief systems could work together when the mission was clear.

The role compressed me. But the environment grew me.

This is the tension leaders must hold. Roles can be limiting and formative at the same time. The question is not whether your current role fully expresses you. The question is whether you are still connected to the identity that exists beyond the role so that when the role ends or changes, you do not collapse with it.

Over the course of your career, the roles you play may expand as step into and grow your talents and abilities. You may then experience a time of contraction, as I did. But whatever role you're playing, pay attention to what's going on in the rooms where you play your roles.

One of the most practical applications of this identity-role distinction is what I call 'the capacity of the room.' It's a principle I live by, and it comes from years of entering rooms where my presence carried more weight than I realized. I had to learn, sometimes painfully, that not every room could hold everything I brought into it.

Here is the principle: you do not have to change who you are when you enter a room. But you must understand the capacity of the people who are in it.

Every person has a capacity for complexity, for depth, for honesty, for challenge, and for nuance. These capacities are not fixed forever; they show up in the moment. Stay present—because when you pour your energy out beyond someone else's capacity, it does not land. It overflows. It creates confusion instead of clarity, resistance instead of resonance.

Imagine filling an eight-ounce cup with water coming out of a 32-ounce bottle. The cup is not defective. It simply cannot hold what you are pouring. The overflow becomes a mess that is not received. It has spilled and someone has to be responsible to clean it up.

This situation happens when leaders enter rooms without discernment.

Early in my pastoral leadership, I did not understand the weight of my presence. I would walk into rooms and be playful, casual, and unguarded because it felt authentic to me. But the people in those rooms usually had a different expectation of my presence. I was their spiritual leader. They expected gravity, not levity. My authenticity, delivered without discernment, created dissonance.

I was not wrong to be myself. I was wrong to ignore the capacity of others whose frameworks were built on wanting only to see me as a solemn leader .

The same dynamic showed up in reverse in other times in my life. When I first entered rooms as an entrepreneur seeking investment, I led with facts, projections, and proofs of concept. I had done all the homework. My numbers were solid. But I failed to read the room. Investors were evaluating my business model. They were evaluating me. They wanted connection before commitment.

Because I had prioritized data over relationship, I did not get the investment.

Years later, I entered a similar room with a different posture. I listened before I pitched. I asked about the investor's story before I told mine. I found the overlap between what he cared about and what I was building. I did not shrink. I did not perform. I discerned. He did not invest that day, but he did open doors. He became a connection. And that connection led to more than any single transaction could have.

That is the principle of 'the capacity of the room' in practice. It is not code-switching. Code-switching is leaving parts of yourself behind to fit in. Knowing 'the capacity of the room' is bringing your full self and stewarding your impact.

Knowing 'the capacity of the room' is not manipulation. Manipulation is adjusting yourself to extract something from people. Knowing 'the capacity of the room' is adjusting your expression to serve people.

When you know 'the capacity of the room,' you are not shrinking. Shrinking makes you smaller because you believe you are too much. Recognize that your fullness must be poured with wisdom—not all at once, and not into every container.

What makes knowing 'the capacity of the room' work well for you? The practice of discernment.

Before you enter a room, your ability to discern asks: "What do I know about this environment? What does this room reward? What does it resist? What is the cultural context? What are the unspoken expectations?"

When you enter the room, you observe and then discern: "Who speaks? Who defers? What language is valued? What topics are welcomed? What topics are avoided? Where is the power? Where is the openness?"

As you engage with those in the room, discernment asks and calibrates: "What can I offer that will land? What should I hold back because the people in that room cannot yet receive it? Where can I be fully present without overwhelming the space?"

A wise mentor once told me: "Study like there is no Holy Spirit. Then get up and teach like you are completely dependent on the Holy Spirit." That counsel applies beyond preaching. It applies to every room you enter. Do your homework. Prepare thoroughly. Know what you carry. And then, when you arrive, stay present. Listen. Adjust. Discern.

This is not performance. This is stewardship.

The I^3 Assessment states: "I adapt my communication style without compromising my integrity." So here are the core questions of discernment: Can you flex without fracturing? Can you adjust without abandoning? Can you be appropriate without becoming invisible?

Leaders who score high on discernment ability know the difference between adaptation and assimilation. They can enter any room—corporate, faith, cross-cultural, high-stakes—and remain coherent. Not because they refuse to adjust, but because their adjustments flow from identity, not from fear.

There is another force that distorts the identity-role relationship. It may surprise you because it often operates in environments where belonging is most valued. That force is loyalty.

Loyalty, in its healthy form, is a virtue. It builds trust. It sustains relationships. It creates the kind of long-term commitment that allows teams, families, and communities to flourish.

But when loyalty becomes a demand rather than a gift, can turn lethal. Lethal loyalty is when a person, system, or leader requires your allegiance at the expense of your alignment. It is when staying faithful means staying silent about what you know is true. It is when belonging requires you to suppress your discernment, ignore your conscience, or betray your values.

Lethal loyalty often arrives disguised as family language: "After everything I have done for you...." and "If you were really with us...." and "I need to know where your loyalty lies."

Those phrases are not always used as manipulation. Sometimes they are simply clumsy attempts at connection. But when they carry an implicit threat—such as when your belonging depends on your compliance—then they become tools of control.

Bishop Cynthia James, Ph.D. names this tension well. She says, "Leaders must find the balance between liberty and loyalty"

Loyalty says: I am committed to this person, this team, this mission.

Liberty says: I am still free to act with integrity, even within that commitment.

When loyalty eclipses liberty, the leader loses agency. They become so invested in belonging that they will sacrifice alignment to keep it. They will swallow concerns. They will enable dysfunction. They will perform agreement while carrying private dissent.

That is not faithfulness. It is fusion.

And fusion—whether to a person, a system, or a role—always erodes identity.

Consider your level of leadership skill by how true you feel this statement is for you : "I lead from conviction rather than approval seeking." Leaders who score low on this item are often caught in loyalty dynamics that have become lethal. They know what they believe, but they have stopped expressing it because the cost of honesty feels too high.

Here is what I want you to hear: you can honor people without surrendering your center. You can be faithful without being fused. You can love deeply and still hold a line.

That is not disloyalty. That is integrity.

Return now to where we began: seeing roles as expressions, not definitions. Remember the client who called me after four years? She was not broken. She was navigating. Her new environment had new expectations, and her roles were shifting. But her identity—the core self she and I had excavated together—was still intact. She had not lost herself. She had temporarily forgotten that her roles were meant to express her, not define her.

That is the reframe this chapter offers. Your roles are real. They carry responsibility. They demand attention. They shape how others experience you. But they are not you.

You are not your title.

You are not your function.

You are not your usefulness.

You are not the version of you that the room rewards.

You are the person beneath all of that; the person who existed before the role arrived and will remain after the role ends.

When you are clear on that distinction, things shift:

You stop defending roles as if they were your identity.

You stop collapsing when roles change.

You stop over-functioning to prove your worth.

You stop confusing loyalty to a system with alignment with your values.

You start leading from identity instead of for identity.

And that shift---from leading for identity to leading from identity is where agency returns.

Here is a practice you can use immediately. Write down your five most active roles right now. Do not overthink it. Just name them. Beside each role, prepare to answer two questions.

The first question is, "What does this role demand from me?"

Demands are external. They include expectations, pressures, visibility, deliverables, emotional labor, time, and energy.

The second question is, "What does this role awaken in me?"

Awakenings are internal. They include gifts, such as your calling, your conviction, your passion, your creativity, and your alignment. When a role demands constantly but rarely awakens, pay attention. That is where role compression lives. That is where exhaustion hides. That is where identity begins to erode.

Now, beneath your answers to those questions, add a third question: "What is the smallest way I have been editing myself in this role?"

Smallest is important because most leaders do not disappear all at once. They disappear by degrees—a softened opinion here, a swallowed concern there, a part of themselves steps aside because the role did not reward it. Name the edit. Because once you name it, you can decide whether to reclaim it.

The information in this chapter was not meant to make you resent your roles. Roles are necessary. They give structure to responsibility. They organize your leadership. They allow you to contribute meaningfully to the people and systems you serve.

The goal is to restore the proper relationship between identity and role.

Identity is the foundation.

Roles are the expressions.

When that order is reversed, when roles become the foundation and identity becomes negotiable, fragmentation follows. You become excellent at delivering what the role demands while quietly losing access to who you are.

When identity is anchored, roles become what they were always meant to be—vehicles for expression, not cages for compression.

You can hold multiple roles without splitting into multiple selves.

You can adapt to different environments without losing coherence.

You can serve people powerfully without disappearing in the process.

That is the fruit of integration.

And when your identity is clear and your roles are properly ordered, something else becomes possible. Your presence begins to carry weight that does not depend on title or position. People trust you before they can explain why. The attitude in the room shifts when you enter them, not because you dominate, but because you are coherent.

That is influence. And that is where we turn next.

A Quiet Declaration

My roles express me. They do not define me. I lead from identity, not for identity. I steward my presence without shrinking my self. I honor people without surrendering my center.

Reflection

- Which role currently has the strongest grip on your sense of worth?
- Where are you most likely to pour beyond the capacity of the room?
- What is one role that demands constantly but rarely awakens?
- Where have you confused loyalty with alignment?
- If you led from identity instead of for identity, what would change first?

CHAPTER 6
LEADING FROM IDENTITY, NOT PERFORMANCE

Performance can produce results. Only identity produces trust.

~Alicia Partee

It was right before my 2024 performance appraisal. We were on Zoom, my manager and I, face-to-face through screens, which is how most of our conversations happened. I'd been thinking about what I wanted to say for weeks, maybe longer. And when the moment came, I did not rehearse. I did not soften. I just said it: "You're not leveraging who I am. This role is not matching how I'm wired and what I've developed."

I was calm. My speech was not forced. It was matter-of-fact. I told him the truth.

When I first came into that organization, it was during a reorganization. I was excited. I thought I would be building something new; a quality function that had never existed before. That was energizing. That was aligned with who I am.

But the role was actually something else. It became maintenance. Repetition. The same audit protocols applied to different clients, over and over. Facility audits required me to observe things my low vision made impossible to observe. There were points of data I could barely see, and they were tracked across systems that did not reward innovation.

I told him all of it. I said, "I'm an innovator. I'm a creator. You're not even getting half of what you could get out of me."

And then I waited.

His response surprised me. He did not push back. He did not minimize. He said, "Don't even worry about the facility audits. I'm close to the sites. I'll do them for you."

He meant it. He did them. He became supportive in ways I did not expect.

Did we solve the problem? No. The role is still compressing. I am still auditing. My gifts are still largely untapped in my day-to-day work. But something shifted in that conversation—not in my circumstances, but in me.

I had led from identity, not performance.

I had named what was true without whining, without demanding, without performing distress to earn sympathy. I'd simply said who I was and told him how my role was not in alignment. And by telling the truth, I reclaimed what the company's performance-based leadership was eroding—my agency.

That is what this chapter is about.

There is a difference between authority and performance, and there are two ways to lead.

The first way of leadership is to shape yourself to the environment. You observe what the room rewards. You study the unspoken rules. You calibrate your presence, your language, your visibility, and your opinions to match what will be accepted, praised, or promoted. You become what the system needs you to be. And because you function at a high capacity, you do it well. You rise. You deliver. You succeed.

That is performance-based leadership. And it works...until it costs you.

The second way is to lead from identity. You enter the room knowing who you are. You adapt your expression without abandoning your core. You speak truth without weaponizing it. You hold your ground without dominating. You remain coherent across environments, not because you refuse to flex, but because your flexing flows from a stable center.

This is identity-based leadership. It is slower to build. It is harder to fake. And it is the only kind of leadership that sustains.

The difference between those two approaches is not always visible from the outside. Both can look competent. Both can produce results. Both can earn respect.

But over time, the difference becomes unmistakable.

Performance-based leaders are exhausted by success. They achieve and feel empty. They deliver and feel unseen. They adapt so often that they lose track of what they actually believe. They are praised for what they do, but they are not known for who they are because they have been hiding themselves in order to keep the praise coming.

Identity-based leaders are sustained by alignment. They hold difficult roles without losing themselves. They navigate compression without collapsing. They speak hard truths without aggression because their worth is not dependent on the room's response. They lead from conviction, not approval.

The I^3 assessment states: "I lead from conviction rather than approval seeking." This is one of the most revealing questions in the profile. Leaders who score low are often highly successful, but their success is held hostage by the need to be affirmed. They cannot take risks that might disappoint. They cannot speak truths that might alienate. They cannot be fully themselves because full selfhood has not been safe.

Leaders who score high on this item have learned to unhook their worth from the room's reaction. They still care about impact. They still want to be effective. But they have stopped performing in order to feel like they belong.

That shift changes everything.

I know what performance-based leadership costs because I lived inside it for years.

In my early career, I was rewarded for delivery. I was praised for results. I was promoted for being the one who could walk into chaos and create order, who could see gaps and fill them, who could exceed expectations and make the system work. That kind of capacity gets celebrated. It also gets exploited.

When you are known for delivering well, people stop asking how you are doing. They assume you are fine. They assume you do not need support. They assume your competence means you are thriving. But sometimes competence is just a very effective mask.

Performance-based leadership taught me to over-function. It taught me to anticipate needs before anyone named them. It taught me to solve problems before anyone else noticed them. It taught me to carry more than my share because carrying it felt safer than asking for help.

And it worked. I advanced. I led. I built.

But I also burned people out—including myself. I ran my home like a business. I scheduled my children into excellence without stopping much to be present with them. I confused doing with loving. I thought showing up meant delivering, when sometimes showing up just means being there.

Performance-based leadership costs you your presence. It costs you your rest. It costs you the kind of intimacy that can only emerge when you stop producing and simply exist.

And performance-based leadership costs you your own voice. When your worth depends on approval, you learn to say what lands instead of what is true. You learn to modulate instead of declare. You learn to manage perception instead of leading from conviction.

That is not leadership. That is survival dressed in a leadership title.

I am in a season right now that is teaching me something I could not have learned during my high-performance years.

My current role—auditing behavioral health programs for Santa Clara County—is not aligned with my strengths. It does not leverage my gift for innovation. It does not invite me to build, create, or reimagine. It is maintenance. It is repetition. It is calibration and compliance and the same protocols applied across different clients.

My husband notices my dissatisfaction, and in fact, I am miserable. He hates watching me navigate it. Honestly, he is not wrong. I do not love the work. I regularly pray for a way out. I have told my manager, clearly and calmly, that this role is not using who I am.

And yet, I am still there. Still showing up. Still stewarding. Why? Because I am learning that I can lead from identity even when the role does not reward it.

In my earlier years, I needed the role to affirm me. I needed the work to be exciting. I needed to over-deliver to feel valuable. If the role did not let me shine, I would have either forced my way into visibility or spiraled into resentment.

Now, I am learning a different posture.

I am learning that my identity does not depend on whether or not playing the role expresses all of me. I am learning that I can be compressed without being erased. I am learning that status quo performance is not failure. It is sometimes simply the honest output of a misaligned season.

I am learning that I can be a good steward of a role I do not love, without pretending to love it, without performing enthusiasm I do not feel, and without letting the role define my worth.

What I just described is identity-based leadership in action. Are the circumstances ideal? No, but the leader is anchored.

Before the reorganization moved me into auditing, I had a different experience in working at Santa Clara County Behavioral Health. I'd been a contract manager, a role that let me do what I do best. I managed relationships with community agencies. I helped them solve problems, find resources, and strengthen their programs. Every agency was different, which meant every day brought new challenges. I was still building. Still identifying gaps. Still innovating.

And my boss trusted me enough to give me a project that used all of me.

She asked me to help create a vision and mission for our division, Adult and Older Adult Services. It was not a small task. It meant working across teams, launching surveys, gathering input, facilitating conversations, and synthesizing everything into language that could guide the organization forward.

I loved it.

We held raffles to encourage participation. We created space for people to dream about what the division could become. We built something together, and the vision and mission we created were adopted and implemented. They are still in use today.

That project was not just a task. It was an expression. It let me be fully who I am: a creator, a builder, a gap-finder, a vision-caster. And it reminded me what becomes possible when identity and role are aligned.

What made my boss trust me with that project? I think it was because I showed up as myself from the beginning. She knew I also had a role being a pastor. She knew what I believed. She knew I was not performing a version of myself to earn her approval. I was simply present, transparent, and ready to contribute. That kind of clarity builds trust faster than any résumé.

The contrast between that season and this one is stark. But both seasons reinforced an essential truth: identity-based leadership is not dependent on ideal conditions. It is a posture you carry into every room, whether the room rewards you or not.

One of the ways identity-based leadership shows up in my current role is through transparency about my physical limitations. Nothing can correct the low vision I experience with nystagmus. And I'm in a role that requires reviewing data points, reading fine print, and conducting facility audits that depend on visual observation.

Could I have hidden my nystagmus? Yes. I could have performed competence and quietly struggled. I could have let things slip through because I was too proud to admit I could not see them. But I didn't hide it. I told my team.

I said, "When we do facility audits, I am not going to see whether there's a rip in the rug or whether the signs are posted correctly. If I'm the one auditing, everyone's going to pass." We laughed about it, but the truth underneath was serious. I cannot do what I cannot do. And pretending otherwise would not serve the work or the people.

My manager stepped in. My colleagues offered to accompany me or cover sites I could not assess. They did not treat my transparency as weakness. They treated it as information and they responded with support.

This is what identity-based leadership makes possible. When you are not performing as though you are invincible you can receive help without feeling shame. When you are not protecting your image, you name your limitations without fear. When your worth is not tied to appearing capable in every domain, you let others contribute where you cannot.

That is not diminished leadership. That is mature leadership.

The I^3 Assessment states: "I can tolerate ambiguity without losing clarity about who I am." Leaders who score high on this item are not threatened by uncertainty—including the uncertainty of their own limitations. They can hold complexity without collapsing. They can admit gaps without spiraling. They can lead confidently while remaining honest about what they do not know or cannot do.

Transparency is not the opposite of strength. It is the evidence of it.

There is another dimension to leading from identity that I must now name, especially for women who lead across multiple domains. Women leaders sometimes have issues with their own visibility.

Visibility is complicated, especially for women leaders who are often evaluated differently than male leaders. Women are praised for collaboration but penalized for authority. Women are expected to be warm but not too soft, strong but not too aggressive, visible but not too ambitious. These rules are unwritten, inconsistent, and exhausting to navigate.

I have been overlooked because I am a woman. I have been told—by a man in a church context—exactly that. He said, “You have to give me time. I’m used to a man’s voice.”

I have watched doors open for men that stayed closed for me, despite my equal or greater qualification. I have wondered, more than once, whether I would already be a lead pastor if I were not female.

These realities are not complaints. They are context. And they shape how women must think about identity-based leadership.

There is a hidden temptation women must overcome. When our visibility is harder to earn, performance becomes more appealing to do. A woman who senses this will work twice as hard to prove she belongs. She shrinks parts of herself to avoid being labeled “too much.” She manages perception so carefully that she loses track of her own voice.

That is not the answer.

The answer is to lead from identity. When a woman leads from identity, she knows that the room may not always reward it, knows that some doors may stay closed, and knows that visibility may come slower or look different than it does for others. But she leads with identity anyway.

Identity-based leadership does not guarantee recognition. It guarantees coherence. And coherence, over time, builds the kind of trust that performance alone cannot manufacture.

In my current role with a county government, I do not feel pressure about being a woman. The environment is professional and equitable.

But in church leadership, the dynamics are different. Some spaces still believe women should not lead. Some voices still question whether a woman’s authority is legitimate. That issue requires another book—one that I am not writing today. This is about leadership. This is about your right to be a leader.

If you are a woman leading in spaces where your visibility is contested, you are not imagining the resistance. The solution is not to perform harder. The solution is to anchor deeper.

Lead from identity. Let the room catch up.

Can a woman who is a leader hold two roles without splitting her energy? Good question, because right now, I hold two leadership roles simultaneously. By day, I am an auditor for Santa Clara County Behavioral Health. On evenings and weekends, I am co-pastor of a church alongside my husband, Dr. Tyrone Partee. The first role compresses me. The second role expresses me. One is paid. The other is not. One is temporary. The other is a calling.

How do I hold both without splitting? The answer is integration. NOTE: I love this

I do not become a different person when I leave the county office and enter the church. I do not perform secularism at work and then perform spirituality at church. I am the same person in both spaces! I am anchored in the same identity, guided by the same values, and I express different facets of who I am depending on what the context requires.

My colleagues at the county know I am a pastor. I do not hide it. I do not broadcast it unnecessarily, but I do not deny it either. When people on call me for a prayer—and they do so throughout both my days and nights—I respond. When my faith informs my perspective, I do not sanitize it. I have boundaries, but I do not have a split self.

This is what the I^3 framework calls integration: the capacity to be the same person everywhere, without assimilation, without fragmentation, without losing yourself to fit the room, the people in that room, and the situation that is going on in that space.

Holding two roles does not require becoming two people. It requires knowing who you are beneath both roles and letting that identity lead.

I've learned—and you will too—what identity-based leadership makes possible. When you lead from identity instead of performance, several things shift. So be prepared.

You can speak truth without aggression. Because your worth is not dependent on the room's approval, you do not need to weaponize honesty to protect yourself. You can say hard things calmly. You can name reality without performing outrage. You can disagree without dominating.

You can receive feedback without collapse. Criticism no longer feels like annihilation. You can hear what is useful, release what is not, and remain standing. Your identity is not up for negotiation in every conversation.

You can hold misaligned seasons without losing yourself. Not every role will express all of you. Not every season will reward your gifts. But when identity is anchored, you can steward even the compressing seasons without being crushed by them.

You can let others see your limitations. Transparency becomes possible because you are not protecting an image. You can ask for help. You can admit what you do not know. You can let others contribute where you cannot.

You can lead without exhausting yourself. Performance-based leadership is depleting because you are constantly producing to earn your place. Identity-based leadership is sustainable because your place is not contingent on production.

All of those situations are the fruits of the work in Part II of this book. Identity, once strengthened and clarified, becomes the foundation for a different kind of leadership—one that does not depend on the room's validation to feel legitimate. And when your identity includes the responsibility of having authority as a leader, your self-knowledge must be strong.

For example, there is a kind of authority that does not announce itself. Have you experienced the authority of quiet presence? The authority embedded in your quiet presence does not demand attention. It does not dominate conversations. It does not need to prove itself in every interaction.

It simply enters the room. And the people in the room become aware.

This kind of authority emerges when identity leads. It is not charisma, though charismatic people can have it. It is not volume, though confident speakers can carry it.

It is presence. Coherence. Trustworthiness.

People trust leaders who are the same person everywhere. They trust leaders who do not perform. They trust leaders whose words match their behavior, whose private values align with their public decisions, whose stability does not depend on circumstances.

This kind of trust is not built through impressive performances. It is built through consistent presence over time. And this is what influence actually is. Not the ability to dominate a room; the ability to shape a room by being fully, coherently, reliably yourself.

A quiet presence is only part of the equation. There is another dimension of influence that many leaders neglect, especially leaders who have been told directly or indirectly, that their voice is too much, too direct, too different, too disruptive.

That dimension is voice. And voice, when it has been muted by culture, gender, or organizational pressure, must be reclaimed before influence can fully emerge.

That is the next place this book will take you.

A Quiet Declaration

I will lead from identity, not for approval. I will speak truth without performing outrage. I will hold misaligned seasons without losing myself. I will let my presence carry more weight than my performance.

Reflection

- Where are you currently performing leadership instead of leading from identity?
- What would it cost you to name, calmly and clearly, what is true about your current role?
- Where have you confused visibility with value?
- What limitation have you been hiding that transparency might actually resolve?
- If your worth were no longer tied to the room's approval, what would you finally say?

CHAPTER 7
YOUR VOICE, UNLEASHED

A leader finds her voice when she no longer needs permission to be coherent.

~ **Alicia Partee**

One day, I answered every question.

It was a practice pitch day for entrepreneurs in Norway. I was sitting in room full of investors, all of whom were men. I was presenting a business I had poured myself into, in which we needed investment to scale. I had graduated from the Founder Institute in Oslo, one of only eight companies out of more than 70 that made it through the intensive, pre-accelerator program. I had been named as a "prime profile" alongside my two co-founders. My pitch deck was polished. My numbers were solid. My answers were clear, confident, and complete.

And when I finished, one of the investors looked at me and said: "I just don't believe you."

There were no follow-up questions. No clarification. No engagement with the substance of what I had presented. Just dismissal.

Some of the people in the room validated me afterward. They told me I had done well. But in that moment, something inside me went quiet. Not because I doubted my preparation. Not because I thought he was right. But because I realized that sometimes, no matter how clearly you speak, no matter how thoroughly you prepare, your voice will not be received.

And that realization—if you are not careful—can mute you.

This chapter is about voice. Not volume. Voice. You must see your voice as your capacity to speak from identity, to communicate with clarity, to be heard without performing, and to remain coherent even when the room does not receive what you carry.

Voice is one of the most fragile dimensions of leadership. It can be silenced by a single sentence. It can be eroded by years of being overlooked, dismissed, or misunderstood. It can be muted by cultures that do not make room for certain kinds of leaders, certain kinds of perspectives, certain kinds of presence.

And yet voice, when it is unleashed—when it flows from integrated identity rather than fragmented performance—becomes one of the most powerful expressions of influence a leader can carry.

But voice gets muted in many ways, and not all of those ways are dramatic.

Sometimes voice is muted by a single moment: a dismissal, a critique, a public correction that lands harder than it should. You walk into a room confident, and you walk out questioning whether you should have spoken at all.

That was how I felt after my first presentation in the Norwegian language. Afterwards, I was I was not learning the language fast enough. In that moment, I silently declared that I would never speak in Norwegian again. I locked my voice in a chest, wrapped it in chains, and told myself I was protecting it.

Protection, taken too far, becomes silence. And silence, sustained too long, becomes erasure.

Sometimes voice is muted by patterns rather than moments. You notice over time that your contributions are not acknowledged. You notice that others repeat what you said and receive credit for it. You notice that when you speak directly, you are labeled aggressive, but when you soften, you are overlooked. The feedback is contradictory and relentless, and eventually you stop trying to calibrate. You just stop speaking.

Sometimes voice is muted by identity. Women, particularly women of color, often navigate environments where their authority is questioned before they open their mouths. The statistics are well documented: all women-led businesses receive a fraction of venture capital funding. Women in leadership are more likely to be interrupted, more likely to have their ideas attributed to others, more likely to be penalized for the same directness that is rewarded in men.

Now, I do not want to make gender issues the centerpiece of this chapter, but I cannot write about voice without naming this reality. Perhaps you are a woman who has been told you were one of the "too"s (too much, too direct, too confident, too fast, too—something that disqualified you). The pressure to shrink, to not be "too," is real. And the work of reclaiming your voice requires naming that pressure before you can resist it.

Sometimes voice is muted by self-judgment. You hear something about yourself—a word, a label, a critique—and instead of evaluating it, you internalize it. You take a magnifying glass to yourself and look for evidence that confirms the criticism.

When I was labeled as being "unorthodox" early in my pastoral journey, I went to the dictionary to look up the word. I needed to know if being called unorthodox was good or bad. And in that search, I learned something about myself. I was allowing someone else's language to define my identity. I was muting my own voice by giving their assessment more weight than my own.

I once facilitated a leadership gathering of executives from multiple countries, men and women at VP and C-suite levels, and other professionals who had relocated internationally and were navigating the complexity of leading across cultures. This conference took place in Germany.

We were discussing conscious leadership and working through frameworks and strategies. Then something unexpected happened. A woman began to cry.

We stopped and she told a story. She had moved to Germany from a country where women did not wear pants. When she arrived, she bought pants for the first time in her life and wore them backwards. Eight weeks had passed before anyone told her about the error.

Eight weeks.

Even though she laughed when she finished the story, her tears were real. What she was naming was not her error. It was the silence. It was the loneliness of navigating a new culture without anyone caring enough to correct her. It was the humiliation of wondering how many times her name had come up at dinner tables as a joke. It was the muting of her voice before she even knew she had one in this new place.

After she finished speaking, something broke open in the room.

One by one, other executives began to share. There were stories of isolation. Stories of trying to fit in and failing. Stories of being dismissed, overlooked, misunderstood. These were leaders who ran companies and departments, who carried significant authority in their organizations, and they had never had a safe space—until that moment—to talk about how hard it had been.

That moment taught me something I carry into every room I enter now: everyone has a voice, but not everyone has been given space to use it.

The power of leadership is only partly in speaking. It is in creating room for others to speak. It is in listening to stories about experiences you yourself have not lived through. It is in making space for voices that have been muted, not because they lacked something, but because the room did not make room for expression.

There is a common confusion in leadership culture where voice is equated with volume. The assumption is that the loudest person in the room has the most influence. We reward assertiveness and mistake it for authority. We celebrate charisma and confuse it with coherence.

But voice is not volume.

Voice is the capacity to communicate from identity. It is the ability to say what is true without performing outrage, to hold a position without dominating, and to be heard without shouting. You do not have to be loud to have a voice. Sometimes you do not even have to speak to have a voice.

I have watched leaders sit quietly in meetings and carry more influence than anyone else in the room not because they were passive but because when they did finally speak, the time was right and their words landed. They had earned trust through consistency. They had built credibility through presence. They did not need to fill space because their silence was not emptiness. It was patience. It was attention. It carried weight.

That weight is what the I^3 framework calls resonance.

Resonance is influence that lands. It is communication that connects. It is voice that is received not because it is loud, but because it is coherent with identity.

When your voice flows from integrated identity, people hear more than your words. They hear your conviction. They sense your alignment. They trust that what you say matches who you are.

When your voice flows from fragmented identity, people read your performance underneath the words you're speaking. They sense the gap between what you are saying and who you are. They may not be able to name it, but they feel it. And trust their erodes.

Resonance cannot be manufactured. It can only be expressed. And it requires the kind of integration I have been building for you throughout this book.

The aspect of your voice becomes even more complex when you lead across cultures.

Different cultures have different norms around directness, around silence, around who is allowed to speak, and when. What is confident in one culture may be aggressive in another. What is respectful in one culture may be passive in another. Navigating those kinds of differences requires discernment. And discernment requires knowing your own voice well enough to adapt without abandoning it.

Americans who travel or live abroad are often perceived as loud. Some of them are but not all. The stereotype flattens reality. What is true is that American communication tends to be more direct, more explicit, more willing to state conclusions upfront. Norwegian communication, by contrast, tends to be more understated, more indirect, more comfortable with silence.

When I lived in Norway, I had to learn to read a different kind of communication. Norwegians say what they mean, but they do not always say everything they mean. There is economy in their language. There is trust that the listener will fill in the gaps. And for someone like me, trained in American directness, that indirectness can feel confusing, even dismissive.

The temptation in cross-cultural leadership is to abandon your voice entirely; to become so focused on fitting in that you lose track of what you actually believe. Or, you might have the opposite experience of to refusing to adapt at all, insisting that your way of communicating is the only legitimate way.

Neither approach works.

The goal is to hold your voice while honoring the room. To adapt your expression without abandoning your identity. To listen deeply enough to understand how communication works in this culture and then to speak in a way that can be received without losing what is true.

That is discernment in action, and it is one of the most sophisticated applications of the I^3 framework.

If I could distill everything I have learned about voice into one practice, it would be this: tell your story and then listen to others tell their stories.

Stories create connection. Stories build trust. Stories humanize leaders who might otherwise be reduced to titles and functions. When you share your story—not your résumé, but your actual experience, your struggles, your transitions, your becoming—you invite others into relationship. You create space for them to do the same.

And when you listen to someone else's story, something shifts. Fear decreases. Understanding increases. The person in front of you stops being a category and becomes a human being with history, with wounds, with gifts, with a voice that deserves to be heard.

I once considered writing a dissertation titled "No One Told Their Story." The premise was simple: so much of what divides us across cultures, organizations, and communities exists because we have not taken time to hear each other's stories. We make assumptions. We project. We fear what we do not understand. But when we sit down and listen, really listen, the distance collapses.

This is why voice matters. Not just your voice. Everyone's voice.

Leadership that unleashes voice is not about becoming the loudest person in the room. It is about becoming the kind of leader who makes room for voices that have been silenced, who listens before speaking, who creates safety for stories to be told.

That kind of leadership changes cultures. It does not just occupy space. It transforms it.

If your voice has been muted by a moment, a pattern, a culture, or by your own self-judgment, it can be reclaimed. But reclaiming your voice is not the same as becoming louder. It is not about forcing yourself to speak when you have nothing to say. It is about reconnecting voice to identity so that when you do speak, your words carry the weight of who you are.

I have learned a lot about reclaiming voice. The first is that you do not need agreement to be heard.

One of the greatest freedoms I've found is releasing the need for people to agree with me. I want to be listened to. I want to be understood. Everybody wants to be listened to and understood—to be truly heard. But now I do not need everyone to share my conclusions.

When you unhook your voice from the need for agreement, you speak with clarity instead of desperation. You can say what is true and let it land where it lands.

Capacity is real. Not everyone can receive what you carry. That is not a judgment! It is a reality. Some people do not have the capacity to hear certain truths. Some rooms cannot hold certain voices. Recognizing this fact doesn't mean you must mute yourself. It is discernment. You can hold your voice and still choose wisely when and where to release it.

Silence is not always about remaining mute. Sometimes the most powerful thing you can do is listen. Sometimes withholding your voice is not weakness; it is wisdom.

The goal is not to speak constantly. The goal is to ensure that when you do speak, it flows from identity rather than fear, from conviction rather than performance.

Stories unlock what arguments cannot. If you want to be heard, tell your story. If you want to understand, listen to someone's story. Stories bypass defensiveness. Stories create intimacy. Stories are the currency of trust.

The I³ Assessment includes questions that reveal your voice patterns. Do you communicate clearly without over-managing perceptions? Do you adapt your style without compromising integrity? Do you lead from conviction rather than approval seeking? These questions reveal whether your voice is flowing from identity or performing for acceptance.

If you score low in these areas, it does not mean you are broken. It means your voice has been compressed. Compression can be reversed.

Voice is not separate from the work you are doing by reading this book. Your voice is an expression of your actions.

When identity is fragmented, voice becomes fragmented. You say different things in different rooms. You perform a confidence you do not feel. You mute parts of yourself to stay safe. Your communication becomes strategic rather than authentic and people sense it, even when they cannot name it.

When your identity is integrated, your voice becomes coherent. You can enter any room and remain yourself. You adapt your expression without abandoning your core. You speak hard truths without aggression because your worth is not dependent on the room's response. Your voice carries weight because it is connected to something stable.

This is what it means to have your voice unleashed. Not to be louder. Not to be more aggressive. Not to dominate every conversation.

Unleashed means unblocked. It means your voice is no longer trapped behind fear, behind performance, behind the need to be accepted. It means you can speak from identity because when you do, people listen.

There is a final dimension of voice that integrated leaders must understand: your voice is not only for yourself.

After you reclaim your voice, you have the capacity to create space for others to find theirs. You become the kind of leader who listens before speaking, who asks questions that draw people out, who makes it safe for stories to be told.

I learned this during my time as president of the Professional Women's Network in Norway. I was leading an organization of extraordinary women.

They were all professionals from around the world who had relocated, who had built careers, who had navigated complexities I could barely imagine. What I discovered was that my role was not primarily to speak. It was to listen, and to create space for their voices to emerge.

When I look back on that season, what moves me most is not what I said. It is what others said because I made room for them to say it. Women who had once felt invisible found their voice in that community. Women who had once been muted by their circumstances began to speak their truth. That network was a place where voices were honored—my voice, and everyone else's.

That is the kind of leadership the I^3 framework produces. Not leadership that dominates. Leadership that unleashes.

When identity is strengthened, when influence is elevated, when voice is unleashed, what remains is the work of living it. Integration is not a concept to understand. It is a practice to embody. It is the daily discipline of showing up as the same person everywhere, of refusing fragmentation, of choosing coherence even when the environment makes coherence costly.

Part IV is about integration—not as theory, but as lived reality. And it begins with learning to navigate code-switching without losing yourself.

A Quiet Declaration

My voice does not require agreement to be valid. I will speak from identity, not for approval. I will listen as deeply as I speak. I will make room for voices that have been silenced. I will let my presence carry more weight than my volume.

Reflection

- Where has your voice been muted—by a moment, a pattern, or your own self-judgment?
- What story have you not told because you assumed no one would listen?
- Where do you confuse volume with voice?
- Whose story do you need to hear before you speak again?
- If your voice were fully unleashed—not louder, but unblocked—what would you say?

PART IV

INTEGRATION — THRIVE EVERYWHERE

CHAPTER 8
STOP CODE-SWITCHING

Integration is not refusal to adapt. It is refusal to disappear.

~ **ALICIA PARTEE**

Then there was the time when I got in trouble for giving children books.

I was working at a childcare center in Norway, and there were some kids there who were exceptionally bright, curious, eager, and ready for more. So, I gave them books to read. Simple picture books. Age-appropriate material. The kind of thing that, in America, would have been celebrated as going above and beyond. Not in Norway.

I was reprimanded for giving children homework.

I stood there, processing. And in that moment, I made a decision that felt like wisdom but was actually something else. I thought, "I will now act like a Norwegian. I will press down the part of me that loves helping people walk in their purpose and reach their full potential. Let me become what this environment rewards."

That decision had a name: code-switching. And it cost me more than I realized at the time.

This chapter is about code-switching. What is it? What does it cost emotionally? Why is integration a better path? Code-switching is about learning to be the same person everywhere without becoming inflexible, culturally insensitive, or blind to context. It is about belonging without erasure.

Code-switching is often discussed in terms of language or culture. It can ask this question: "Depending on the environment, must you shift how you speak, how you dress, or how you present yourself?" Your answer for this question will vary. Sometimes yes, sometimes no. And sometimes, maybe.

There is a version of self-adjustment that is healthy. Adapting your communication style to be understood is not self-betrayal. Reading a room and having to adjust your approach is not weakness. Knowing when to make an adjustment is wisdom in action.

But that is not what I mean by code-switching.

Code-switching, as I define it, is when you stop being the authentic you and become a version of yourself that is tolerable for others. It is when you pick up cues from the environment and assimilate with them, not because you are adapting from a grounded center, but because you are abandoning yourself to make others comfortable.

Code-switching is about deleting your essence; it is not about making a momentary adjustment in order to navigate the circumstances that you're confronting in the moment.

When you code-switch, you become a person who is acceptable rather than a person who is authentic. You switch into the code of who it is you think they want. You perform belonging instead of experiencing it. And over time, you lose track of who you actually are beneath all the versions you have created.

That is why code-switching is so dangerous for leaders.

A code-switch may not feel like betrayal in the moment. It will feel like a strategy. It may feel like survival. It feels like the smart thing to do in a room that does not reward your full self.

But every time you code-switch, you reinforce an internal message: who you are is not acceptable. And that message, repeated enough times across enough environments, fragments your identity.

Leaders need awareness of the difference between code-switching and understanding the capacity of the room.

Earlier, I introduced a principle I called 'the capacity of the room.' It must be distinguished as separate from code-switching, because the two can look similar on the surface.

Understanding 'the capacity of the room' means that you've used discernment. It begins with knowing who you are; being grounded in your identity before you enter any space. Then it involves several observations: What can this room hold? What is the capacity of the people here? What can I share, how should I share it, and what boundaries do I need to honor?

The capacity of the room does not require you to become someone else. It requires you to steward yourself wisely.

In contrast, code-switching begins with the environment itself. It asks: Who do they need me to be? What version of myself will be accepted here? What parts of me should I hide to fit in?

Do you see the difference?

Capacity of the room says: "I know who I am, and I will share myself appropriately."

Code-switching says: "I do not know if who I am is acceptable, so I will become what they want."

One preserves identity. The other erodes it.

One adapts from strength. The other assimilates from fear.

One leads to integration. The other leads to fragmentation.

The goal of this chapter—and this entire section of the book—is to help you stop code-switching and start practicing integration. Not rigidity. Not cultural blindness. Not the arrogance of refusing to adapt, but the grounded confidence of knowing who you are and then carrying that identity into every room you enter.

Code-switching always costs something. The currency varies among energy, authenticity, peace, and trust, but the exchange is never free.

When I decided to "act like a Norwegian" at that childcare center, I was not just adjusting my behavior. I was pressing down a core part of who I was: someone who loved helping people reach their full potential. That part of me did not disappear. It just went underground. And suppressed identity eventually leaks out as frustration, resentment, exhaustion, or quiet grief.

Code-switching extracts costs from your emotional energy. Maintaining a performance is work. When you are constantly monitoring yourself by editing before you speak, softening before you act, and calibrating before you contribute, you are burning fuel that could be used for actual leadership. The cognitive load of performing is enormous, even when you do not consciously notice it.

Code-switching costs you trust. People sense inauthenticity, even when they cannot name it. When you code-switch, there is a gap between who you are and who you present. That gap creates distance. It makes connection harder. It undermines the trust that integrated leadership builds naturally.

Code-switching is paid for from your own account of clarity. The more versions of yourself you create, the harder it becomes to remember which one is real. Leaders who code-switch across multiple environments often report a strange kind of disorientation in being successful everywhere, but clear nowhere. They have so many selves that they have lost access to the self.

And perhaps most significantly, code-switching costs you in terms of belonging. Not surface belonging; you can code-switch your way into acceptance. It costs in terms of deep belonging, the kind that does not require performance, the kind that comes from being known and still welcomed. Code-switching trades that for a counterfeit: inclusion based on a version of you that is not actually you.

One of the environments where I learned the most about code-switching and its costs was at the intersection of corporate leadership and church leadership.

I spent years in corporate environments where performance, metrics, and outcomes were the currency. I was good at that. I could track numbers, deliver results, and drive projects forward. When I joined the board at my church as treasurer, those skills served me well. I spent seven years of managing finances, building systems, creating accountability.

But when I transitioned into pastoral ministry, those same instincts became liabilities.

Ministry, at least in the contexts I served, was about being people-focused in ways that corporate rarely was. And because I led with numbers and outcomes, people felt I did not care about them. Some thought I was untouchable. Others thought I was unrelatable. The very qualities that made me effective in one environment made me suspect in another.

I tried to adjust. I tried to soften. I tried to "dumb down" the strategic, results-oriented part of myself so I would fit the expectations of what a pastor should be.

It never lasted. Because I am who I am. And eventually, I would 'bust out." The real me would surface, and I would be right back where I started.

What I learned from that season is that code-switching is not sustainable. You can suppress yourself for a time, but you cannot erase yourself permanently. The authentic you will always find a way through. The question is whether it emerges as integration or as explosion.

The reverse was also instructive. When I moved from church leadership back into corporate environments, I sometimes found myself pastoring people I should have simply been working with. The nurturing instincts, the care for people's souls, the desire to walk with them through difficulty—those instincts did not turn off just because I was in a secular setting.

And I realized that maybe they were not supposed to turn off.

Maybe the goal was not to be a different person in church than in corporate. Maybe the goal was to be the same person—adapting my expression, honoring the context—and never abandoning my core.

Be the same person everywhere.

That phrase has appeared throughout this book, and now it is the thesis of Part IV.

Being the same person everywhere does not mean you never adjust. It does not mean you walk into every room with the same volume, the same approach, the same disregard for context. That would be arrogance, not integration.

Being the same person everywhere means your identity stays intact across environments.

You are authentically you, unapologetically you, always. Not because you refuse to adapt, but because your adaptations flow from a grounded center rather than a fragmented fear.

Being the same person everywhere means you do not delete yourself to belong. You do not dim your light to make others comfortable. You do not perform a version of yourself that you will not recognize later. It means you show up at the capacity of the room being fully yourself, wisely expressed, and you let the room respond however it will.

Here is what being the same person everywhere looks like for me in practice:

I am a pastor.

I am a leader.

I am a teacher.

I am a trainer.

I am all of those things, everywhere I go. I do not wave titles. I do not demand recognition. But I also do not pretend those identities do not exist just to make someone else comfortable. I am same person everywhere I go. I am the same person everywhere not out of rigidity. I am the same person everywhere I go because of coherence.

One of the most powerful reframes in the I³ framework is learning how you can belong without being erased.

So much of code-switching comes from a fear that belonging requires erasure, that you must delete parts of yourself to be accepted, that the price of inclusion is invisibility. And in some environments, that fear is not unfounded. There are rooms that will not accept your full self. There are spaces that reward only certain versions of you.

But here is something significant I've learned: belonging that requires erasure is not actually belonging. It is tolerance. It is conditional acceptance. It is a transaction where you trade your authenticity for access.

True belonging—the kind that sustains you, the kind that integrates rather than fragments—happens when you are fully yourself and still welcomed.

I experienced this when I pastored the American Lutheran Congregation in Oslo. It was a church of diplomats and internationals, people from around the world who came to worship in English. The congregation wanted to be interdenominational and international, a place where diverse expressions of faith could come together.

One year, we decided to do something that had never been done there before: a liturgical dance for Easter Sunday. The dancers were from South Africa, America and Poland. I reviewed the choreography and costumes to make sure everything was appropriate. And on Easter morning, they danced.

It was beautiful.

Afterwards, as I stood at the door shaking hands, one man told me it was the worst Easter presentation he had ever experienced.

In an earlier season of my life, that comment would have crushed me. I would have questioned my judgment. I would've wondered if I had made a mistake. I might have code-switched and pulled back from creative expression. I might have played it safer by producing a different Easter event. I might have been more "acceptable."

But I did not. When I'd heard that comment, I understood something that I had not understood before.

This man's discomfort was not about the dance. It was about the unfamiliar. He had encountered something outside his experience, and he did not know what to do with it. But the church had claimed to want international, interdenominational expression. These dancers were expressing the same faith to the same God, just in a different form.

I belonged in that moment not because everyone else approved, but because I was being who I was called to be. I was not erased by his disapproval. My identity remained intact.

Years later, I was on a train in Norway when a woman from that congregation, someone who'd been to that Easter service, recognized me and approached. She said, "You are the only person who taught us about the presence of God. I will never forget that."

Within the space of those two comments, I felt the validation of belonging without erasure. I had not been seeking universal approval of the plan I'd brought forth. Universal approval is impossible and not even desirable. But the deep knowledge that I'd showed up as myself, held my ground, and made a difference outlasted momentary discomfort...and then another person gave me the blessing of a comment that outweighed the critique.

While having faith in God can help with integration of the self, for some leaders whose identity is grounded in faith, code-switching poses a particular threat.

If you believe that God created you with intention—wired you a certain way, shaped you through specific experiences, gifted you for particular purposes—then code-switching goes beyond a leadership problem. It is a theological problem.

How can you say that God made you to be and do and contribute in a certain way, but then refuse to hold to your God-given identity when the environment gets uncomfortable? How can you claim to trust the Creator's design while constantly editing that design to fit human expectations?

This is where a deeper understanding of faith and vocation becomes essential.

You are more than a leader. You are the church. Not the building. You are part of its body. Wherever you go, you carry something sacred. Your sphere of influence, whether it is a boardroom, a neighborhood, a classroom, or a family dinner table, is your pulpit. You do not leave your faith at the door of secular spaces. You bring it with you not as performance, not as imposition, but as presence.

That reframe has changed how I think about integration.

I do not draw lines between what is sacred and what is secular, between church and corporate, or between ministry and marketplace. I see them as false divisions. I am the same person everywhere because I carry the same identity everywhere.

My faith does not code-switch. My calling does not fragment. My purpose does not change depending on who is watching.

With my neighbors, I am the same person I am at church. I have prayer walks with some of them. With others, I simply ask how they are doing. With some, I offer to pray for specific needs. With others, I just show up and listen. The expression varies. The identity does not.

That is integration. It is not uniformity of expression; it is coherence of identity.

Stopping code-switching is not a one-time decision. It is dynamic. It is a daily practice.

Every time you enter a new environment, you face two questions. Will you perform what the room rewards? Will you show up as who you are and trust that your presence has value?

There are practices that support integration over code-switching.

Ground yourself before you enter a room. Before walking into any significant environment, take a moment to remember who you are beyond your title, your role, and your identity. Tap into the core self that exists beneath what you do. When you enter from that grounded place, you are less likely to be destabilized by the room's expectations.

Observe before you adjust. Adaptation is not the enemy. Unconscious assimilation is. What are the norms there? What does the room reward? What is the capacity of the people gathered there? Then make conscious choices about how to express yourself—choices that honor the context without abandoning your core.

When you feel adjustment is necessary, give a name to what you must edit in yourself. When you notice yourself softening, shrinking, or deleting parts of yourself, pause. Then name it. Ask, "What am I hiding? Why? Is this wisdom, or is this fear?"

Sometimes the edit is appropriate because not every room needs every part of you. But often the edit is code-switching in disguise. Naming it lets you avoid it by making you aware that underneath the change in your behavior or attitude, the real you still exists in the temporary shadow of the situation.

Accept the costs of coherence. Integration is not free. Some rooms will not accept you as your full self. Some people will be uncomfortable with your authenticity. Some opportunities may close because you refused to perform a role that was not entirely authentic. Those are the costs. And they are worth paying, because the alternative—fragmentation—costs much more in the long run.

Celebrate small integrations. Every time you show up as yourself and the world does not end, you build evidence that integration is possible. Notice those moments. Celebrate them. Let them become the foundation for larger acts of coherence.

I want to be clear about what this chapter is not saying. Integration is not rigidity.

To stop code-switching does not mean to stop adapting. It does not mean that you should barrel into every room with the same approach, regardless of context. It does not mean you can ignore cultural differences, dismiss feedback, or refuse to grow.

Integration is flexible—and beneficial. Having a rigid mindset about integration is inflexible—and harmful.

Integrated leaders read rooms. They honor cultures. They adjust their communication to be understood. They listen before they speak. They learn from environments that are different from what they know.

But they do all of this from a stable center. They adapt their expression without abandoning their essence. They flex without fragmenting.

Your decision goes a bit beyond whether or not to adapt. Will you keep your identity while you adapt or will you abandon your identity while you adapt? That question, asked and answered honestly, is the practice of integration.

Integration becomes even more complex when you lead across different organizational cultures as well as different national cultures—all with different values, different communication styles, and different assumptions about leadership itself. That is where cultural intelligence meets identity. And that is where I'm taking you next in this book.

A Quiet Declaration

I will stop performing versions of myself to earn belonging. I will adapt my expression without abandoning my essence. I will show up as the same person everywhere---not rigid, but coherent. I will belong without being erased.

Reflection

- ➤ Where have you code-switched so often that you forgot it was a performance?
- ➤ What part of yourself do you most often delete to make others comfortable?
- ➤ Where have you experienced belonging that required erasure---and what did it cost you?
- ➤ If you showed up as the same person everywhere, what would you stop hiding?
- ➤ What would it mean for your faith if you stopped drawing lines between sacred and secular?

CHAPTER 9
CULTURAL INTELLIGENCE MEETS IDENTITY

Thriving globally is not flexibility of identity.
It is clarity of self with skillful navigation.

~ **Alicia Partee**

If you ever visit Norway, you will learn that only three kinds of people say hello to strangers on the bus: those who are drunk, those who are mentally unstable, and Americans.

I was that American.

I'd board a bus, smile at the people around me, and say hello—exactly the way I had done my entire life in California. I was always met with silence. People averted their eyes and I witnessed the quiet, polite discomfort of people who did not understand why a stranger was speaking to them.

It was not rudeness on my part. It was my culture. In Norway, public space is private space. You do not impose yourself on strangers. You do not assume familiarity. You wait to be invited into connection.

I did not know that so I kept saying hello. And people kept looking at me like I had lost my mind.

Those small moments—ones I repeated dozens of times over the years—are what taught me something important about cultural intelligence. It is not enough to know about a culture. You have to know its people. And people, even within the same culture, are not all the same.

This chapter is about the intersection of cultural intelligence and anchored identity. It is about learning to navigate diverse environments without losing yourself. It is about the difference between assimilation, which erases you, and integration, which expands you. And it is about why thriving globally requires clarity of self first—long before flexibility of identity.

What is cultural intelligence? Often called CQ (as in Cultural Quotient), cultural intelligence is typically defined as the capability to function effectively across national, ethnic, and organizational cultures. It involves understanding cultural norms, adapting behavior appropriately, and building relationships across difference.

That definition is accurate. It is also incomplete.

I define cultural intelligence because of the way I learned it. Culture is a person. Intelligence is hearing a person's story and understanding it, but not necessarily agreeing with it.

This definition reframes the matter because traditional approaches to cultural intelligence can be another form of performance. For example, you study the culture. You learn the norms. You adapt your behavior. And if you are not careful, you become so focused on fitting in that you forget to show up as yourself.

Cultural intelligence without having anchored your own identity produces chameleon-like leaders who can blend into any environment but who have lost track of who they actually are.

I have seen this pattern repeatedly in my work with globally mobile leaders who have high CQ, but low identity clarity. They can read any room. They can adapt to any culture. They know the right things to say and the right ways to behave. And they are exhausted. They feel inauthentic. They feel invisible. They feel lonely even in crowded rooms. Every time they encounter something admirable in another culture, they try to become it.

They morph. They assimilate. They lose a little more of themselves with each adaptation.

Cultural intelligence is essential for global leadership. But cultural intelligence without identity is just sophisticated code-switching. And code-switching, as we explored in the last chapter, always costs more than it gives.

I once saw a TV commercial in Norway for the Telia telecommunications company. The image was an assembly line, a conveyor belt carrying people who all looked exactly the same. Same posture. Same expression. Same conformity. Then one person got on the belt who was different. That person disrupted the uniformity. They stood out. And according to the commercial, they made everything better.

That image stayed with me because it captured exactly what assimilation produces as well as what it costs.

Assimilation is the process of becoming indistinguishable from the dominant culture. You erase the parts of yourself that do not fit. You adopt the norms, the values, the behaviors of your environment until you blend in completely. You become acceptable by becoming invisible.

And there is the problem: when everyone looks the same, everyone produces the same. Innovation dies. Creativity stalls. The very diversity that makes teams and organizations stronger gets smoothed away in the name of belonging.

Assimilation is often taught as the goal of cultural adaptation. Fit in. Blend in. Do not stand out. But assimilation is not integration. Assimilation requires you to disappear. Integration allows you to belong while remaining yourself.

Authentic integration—the kind I teach and the kind this book is about—means understanding who you are and intentionally navigating new cultures without changing your core. You adapt your expression. You learn the norms. You honor the context. But you do not delete yourself to do it.

When I realized that assimilation was not working because it was costing me more than it was giving me, I built an entire company around the alternative. I called it Authentigrate—a combination of the words 'authentic' and 'integration.' The name captured my goal to help leaders integrate into new environments without losing their authenticity.

Here's a story about a client I worked with in Norway.

He was from the United Kingdom; highly intelligent, accomplished, operating at an executive level. He commanded teams of teams, leaders of leaders. His performance metrics were excellent. By any external measure, he was succeeding.

But when he came to see me, something was wrong.

He could not map who he was going to be in this new space. He had relocated internationally, and despite his professional success, he felt disconnected from himself. He was performing well—hitting numbers, leading meetings, delivering results—but he did not know who he was underneath the performance. He had high cultural intelligence and low identity clarity.

We worked together using evidence-based practices alongside the I³ framework. We excavated his overall identity—both his professional identity and his core self. We explored what grounded him, what he valued, what remained constant across environments. We built a foundation that could hold his leadership without requiring him to fragment.

The change was measurable. And it was visible.

By the time I left Norway, he was a different man. Not different in the sense of becoming someone new, but different in the sense of becoming more fully himself. He was less lonely. Less conflicted. He knew who he was and what he was worth. If you have ever seen a movie where scales fall off someone's eyes and they emerge transformed, that was him.

He did not leave his role. He did not abandon his cultural adaptations. But he stopped letting those adaptations erase him. He led from identity, not for acceptance. And that shift changed everything.

When you move to a new country, your identity gets tested in ways you do not anticipate.

The obvious challenges are logistical: language, transportation, housing, employment. But the deeper challenges are existential. Questions arise: "Who am I in this place?" and "How do I translate who I was into who I am becoming?" and "Where do I belong when the rules have changed and no one knows my history?"

The most common struggle I see in globally mobile leaders is culture shock that becomes identity shock. The external change triggers an internal transition, and if the leader does not have a strong identity foundation, they will assimilate their way through it and lose themselves in the process.

I would not have survived my years in Norway without the international community. My mentor was from the Czech Republic. My teachers were Norwegian. My board included leaders from the countries of Georgia, America, Russia, and the United Kingdom. My business partners were from Egypt and Afghanistan.

Those relationships taught me that cultural intelligence is more than mastering a single culture. It is about listening to individual stories, personal stories, the kinds of stories that textbooks and training programs cannot capture.

People are more than their nationality, their accent, their cultural background. They carry personal values, personal experiences, personal wounds, and personal gifts. And when you take time to hear those stories, fear decreases as connection increases. The person in front of you stops being a representative of their culture and becomes a human being you can actually know.

Cultural intelligence in its truest form is the ability to forge understanding of and intimacy with all types of people.

The expatriate experience taught me many lessons and shaped my identity in important ways. It led to starting a company to address the need for self and cultural intelligence. It led to writing this book.

Living as an expatriate tested my identity. Then when I moved back to Norway, repatriation broke it open.

When I returned to America after years in Norway, I expected the transition to be easy. I was going home, back to California. Back to sunshine and familiar faces and the culture I'd grown up in and knew so well. I thought I would slide back into my old life as if putting on a comfortable jacket.

I was so wrong.

The reverse culture shock was worse than the original culture shock. I stood in a SuperTarget and cried because there were too many choices. I tried to tell stories about Norway and people said, "But you're back in America now." I reached out to the international community for support and they said, "You're an American in America. You're not international anymore.'

I felt that I did not fit anywhere.

It wasn't because I had changed in ways that made me unrecognizable. It was because I had grown in ways that my old environment could not hold. The people who knew me before did not have the capacity to receive all I had become. And that was not their fault. It was simply reality.

Repatriation taught me something that expatriation could not teach—that identity is not about nationality. It is not about where you are from or where you live. Identity morphs as a human response to change. And whenever change happens—whether you are moving abroad or coming home—you have to do the work of finding your belonging and becoming.

I found my way through intentional community. I joined Lisa Nichols's Motivating the Masses program and found a tribe of people committed to growth. And then I found Cindy Trimm, Ph.D., creator of the SOAR mentoring program. When I enrolled in it, I found a space that encompassed all of me.

And I kept becoming, because becoming never stops.

Here is what I tell leaders who are about to repatriate: be ready. Be ready for people not to have the capacity to receive all that you have received and all that you have become. And make decisions for yourself based on that reality. Do not shrink to fit the old, familiar spaces. Find new spaces that can hold the person you have become.

The world is full of diversity beyond its inhabitants. There are different geographic features, time zones, ecosystems, genetics, and fauna and flora. And there are differences in leadership styles and attitudes.

I once had the opportunity to work with a Fortune 100 company in Scandinavia on a diversity and inclusion initiative. They wanted to build high-performing teams across cultural differences so they brought me in to facilitate.

We started with the creation of teams who would create focus groups, surveys, and curricula for workshops to teach leaders how to truly understand the cultural background and identity of each individual on their team. Their stories. The unique contribution they could lend. The overall purpose was to explore how different identities and behaviors could work together rather than against each other.

Our work was well received. It expanded from one team to the entire organization. I received recognition for the impact.

But here is an issue the project revealed—the people who needed the most help were not the team members. They were the leaders.

As you rise in an organization, the numbers get thinner. There are fewer peers. Fewer safe spaces. Fewer people you can talk with about the challenges of leading diverse teams while maintaining your own identity. Leaders at the top often have nowhere to go with their questions about cultural intelligence, identity, or how to hear the stories of every unique individual while staying balanced themselves.

That realization shifted my focus. I began concentrating on the leaders—and the leaders of the leaders. I felt that if I could help a leader integrate their own identity, then they would create space for everyone beneath them to do the same.

Integration cascades.

What happens when a leader enters a global environment without clarity of self?

They assimilate with whoever talks to them first. The first person who shares their perspective is where the leader begins to adapt. Then they discover that person they aligned with is the one everyone else has problems with. So, they talk to the next person and adapt again. Eventually they reach the quiet person—the one who actually understands what is going on—but by then, the leader has been assimilating so constantly that they no longer know who they are.

They overcompensate.

Someone may have mentioned that the last leader did something poorly, so this new leader swings to the opposite extreme.

Someone may have expressed a preference, and this leader caters to it without discernment.

They become reactive instead of grounded.

They never get known. The team was probably given that leader because of who they were and what good change they could bring, but the team never got to experience the truth of that leader's identity because he or she was too busy becoming what everyone seemed to want.

What happens when a leader enters a global environment with clarity of self?

They drink information in by sips, not floods. They share themselves gradually, observing, listening, calibrating. They get feedback and they adjust, but their adjustments are to their expressions, not to their innate essence.

They stay curious without becoming shapeless. They take time to learn the culture, to listen to stories, and to adapt their approaches while maintaining a stable center that the team can trust.

They bring what they were chosen to bring. The team gets the benefit of this leader's actual gifts, their actual perspective, their true identity. And that is what makes the difference.

Thriving globally does not require flexibility of identity. It requires flexibility of expression grounded in clarity of self.

As for my own self-development and identity, living in Norway taught me that America does not have everything.

That is not so much criticism as it is liberation. I grew up believing, as many Americans do, that we had figured things out; that our way was the best way, or at least the default way. But when I lived abroad, I discovered that other cultures had wisdom we lacked, approaches Americans had never considered, and lived values that challenged and expanded my own.

Work-life balance in Norway is not a slogan. It is a practice. People left work at reasonable hours. They took vacations without guilt. They prioritized presence over productivity in ways that initially confused me...and eventually convicted me.

The international community showed me that the world is the best of everything. Every culture carries gifts. Every people group has wisdom. And when you approach cultural differences with curiosity instead of judgment, you become richer. You do not need to abandon your identity—you expand it.

This expansion is what cultural intelligence makes possible when it is paired with anchored identity. You can learn from other cultures without losing yourself. You can adapt without assimilating. You can belong without erasing.

The lessons I learned abroad, I brought home. I listen to people now, whether they've lived internationally or not, because I know that everyone has a story worth hearing. I do not assume I understand someone because I share their nationality. I lean in. I ask questions. I let their uniqueness surprise me.

That posture is cultural intelligence at its best. Not expertise about cultures. Humility

Authentigrate: The Integration Alternative is the name of my company because when I realized that assimilation was failing leaders by costing them their identity, energy, and their effectiveness, something needed to be done. Authentigrate exists to help organizations support their employees and family members as they adjust to new countries and cultures. We work with globally mobile leaders through a program called Cultural Navigator Training, equipping them with the tools to integrate authentically rather than assimilate anxiously.

The name says it all: Authentigrate. Authentic integration. Showing up as yourself in every environment. Belonging without erasure. Adapting without abandoning. And this is the work I am called to. Not because I figured it out with ease, but because I lived the cost of getting it wrong. I know what it feels like to delete yourself to fit in. I know what it costs to assimilate. And I know what becomes possible when you finally anchor your identity and lead from that place.

If you want to learn more about this work, please visit authentigrate.com or authentigrate.ai. But more important than any program is the posture this chapter invites you to hold—and that is having cultural intelligence grounded in identity. Learning without losing. Adapting without assimilating. Becoming without disappearing.

You have now explored all three dimensions of the I^3 framework. Your identity has been strengthened. Your influence has been elevated. Your integration has been practiced. What remains is the question of sustainability. How do you live what you've learned? And I do not mean that you should live it as a concept you understand, but as a daily posture you embody.

The final chapter is about your I^3 life and how to live as authentically integrated for the long haul.

A Quiet Declaration

I will learn cultures without losing myself. I will hear stories without abandoning my own. I will adapt my expression while anchoring my identity. I will belong without erasing. I will thrive globally by knowing who I am.

Reflection

- Where have you confused cultural adaptation with identity abandonment?
- Whose story do you need to hear more fully before you judge their culture?
- What did you learn in a different environment that your home culture could not teach you?
- If you returned home today, what growth would people struggle to receive?
- What would it look like to pour yourself in sips rather than floods?

CHAPTER 10
YOUR I^3 LIFE — LIVING INTEGRATED

You have permission to live as one whole person everywhere God sends you.

~ **Alicia Partee**

You have come a long way.

When you opened this book, you may have been exhausted in ways that did not match your workload. You may have felt fragmented across roles, environments, and expectations—successful everywhere, clear nowhere. You may have been performing versions of yourself without remembering which one was real.

Now you have the language.

You understand what fragmentation costs. You know the difference between identity and roles, between code-switching and capacity of the room, between assimilation and integration. You have seen how strengthened identity becomes the foundation for elevated influence, and how both lead to the possibility of living as the same person everywhere.

But understanding is not the same as living.

This final chapter is about the bridge between knowing and becoming. It is about moving from concept to practice, from insight to posture, from a book you read to a life you embody.

Integration is not a destination you arrive at. It is a way of living you practice daily, intentionally, imperfectly, and persistently.

This is your I^3 life. And it begins now.

I want to be honest with you about something: I am still becoming.

After everything I have shared in this book—the transitions, the lessons, the frameworks, the transformations—I am not finished. I am still practicing integration. I am still learning what it means to be the same person everywhere. I am still growing.

My husband will tell you that I can still seem cold sometimes. When I am tired, when pressure builds, I can slip into functioning mode and manage the household, execute tasks, and get things done without actually connecting with people. I can be present in body and absent in spirit. I can do without being.

I do not like to live that way. So, I practice. I catch myself. I course-correct. I choose connection over completion, presence over productivity—not perfectly—but intentionally.

With my grandchildren, I am learning to simply be there. To sit on the floor and play. To listen without multitasking. To give them my eyes and my attention, not just my schedule because I will not get that time again. And because being present with them is part of being integrated. I bring the same person into the living room that I bring into the boardroom.

Integration is not about arriving at a place where you no longer struggle. It is about developing the awareness to notice when you drift and having the discipline to return to center.

If you expected this book to give you a formula that eliminates the work, I have failed you. But if you expected this book to give you a framework that makes the work possible, I believe I have delivered.

The work is yours now. Stay grounded, and it will last the rest of your life.

People often ask what I do to stay grounded. They want to hear about my practices, habits, and my routines. They want to hear something they can replicate for themselves.

I hesitate to be prescriptive because what works for me may not work for you. Integration is personal. It must be built from the inside out, not imposed from the outside in. That is why discovery matters more than prescription, and why the work I do with leaders always begins with excavation rather than instruction.

But I will tell you what anchors me. It starts with staying in the Word of God. That is my foundation. Scripture reminds me who I am when the world wants to tell me otherwise. It grounds me in an identity that does not shift with circumstances, does not depend on approval, and does not fragment under pressure. When I lose my way, I return there first.

If you do not share my faith, find something else that can ground you. Find a source, such as a self-help book or video, or a practice such as meditation, that takes you to your core when environments ask you to edit yourself. Find a practice that reconnects you to yourself when the roles you've committed to play end up consuming you. Integration requires that you have a foundation—something stable to hold steady you above the shifts.

Beyond that, I practice what Cindy Trimm, Ph.D. calls "me moments." These are times set aside for presence instead of productivity. For me, it's time with God. Time with myself. Time to stay aware, stay connected, stay grounded. Time to be intentional rather than reactive.

Intentionality is the thread that runs through all your "me moments."

Integration does not happen by accident. You do not drift into coherence. You must choose it daily, repeatedly, and in the small moments that no one sees as well as in the large decisions that everyone watches.

The practices themselves matter less than the posture behind the practice. Are you being intentional about your formation? Are you paying attention to your own becoming? Are you building a life that supports integration rather than undermines it? Your answers to those questions matter more than any specific habit I could recommend.

And now I offer you something practical. It's not a rigid plan. It's a posture you can hold for the next 90 days. Think of it as an extended invitation to live what you have learned. Ninety days is enough time for new patterns to take root. It is a time period long enough to move you from understanding into embodiment. During this 90-day practice, you will notice where you drift and where you hold steady.

This is not a curriculum. It is an inventory. A rhythm. A way of paying attention.

Days 1-30: Know Yourself

The first 30 days are about excavation. Take an inventory of who you are, not who you perform, not who others expect you to be, but who you actually are beneath the roles.

Examine your gifts, your talents, your natural capacities. What comes easily to you that others find difficult? What energizes you even when it costs effort? What have you carried since childhood that still shows up in your leadership?

Examine your experiences. What transitions have shaped you? What wounds have formed you? What victories have marked you? Is there a common thread running through your story? Is there a pattern that reveals something about your purpose?

Examine your roles. Which ones express your identity? Which ones compress it? Where do you feel aligned? Where do you feel fragmented?

This is not assessment in the formal sense. It is reflection. Journaling. Conversation with trusted people who know you well. It is taking the time to know yourself deeply enough that you can carry yourself consistently.

Days 31-60: Notice Your Patterns

The second 30 days are about awareness. Now that you have taken inventory, watch how you actually live.

Notice where you code-switch. Notice where you dim your light. Notice where you delete parts of yourself to fit environments that do not reward your fullness.

Notice where you stay grounded. Notice which relationships support your integration. Notice which environments allow you to be the same person you are everywhere else.

Notice without judgment. The goal is not to shame yourself for fragmentation. The goal is to see clearly so you can choose differently.

Keep a simple log to help you remember what you've noticed. At the end of each day, ask yourself questions like: "Where was I fully myself today?" and "Where did I fragment?" and "What triggered the shift?" and "What would I do differently?"

Awareness precedes change. You cannot integrate what you cannot see.

Days 61-90: Practice Integration

The final 30 days are about intentional practice. You know who you are. You have noticed your patterns. Now you begin choosing differently.

Pick one environment where you typically fragment and practice showing up whole. Not perfectly. Not without fear. But intentionally. Bring your full self into a space where you usually edit, and see what happens.

Pick one relationship where you have been performing and practice being present. Let someone see you without the mask. Risk being known rather than being impressive.

Pick one role that has been compressing you and practice expressing your identity through it rather than losing your identity inside it.

Integration is built through small, repeated choices. Each time you choose coherence over fragmentation, you strengthen the muscle. Each time you show up as yourself without any fears, you gather evidence that integration is possible.

After 90 days, you will not be finished. But you will be different. You will have moved from concept to practice, from knowing to becoming.

Why does this 90-day plan work? Evidence!

I have watched leaders transform through this work.

I have seen executives who commanded teams of teams but could not locate themselves beneath the performance. I have seen them excavate their identity, anchor their foundation, and emerge less lonely, less conflicted, more fully alive.

I have seen globally mobile professionals who had assimilated so thoroughly they forgot who they were before they relocated. I have seen them reclaim their core and learn to belong without erasure.

I have seen pastors who felt they were not "spiritual enough," entrepreneurs who were told they were "too much," women leaders who had been shrinking for so long they forgot they could stand at full height. I have seen them straighten, speak, and lead from identity rather than for approval.

What do they say when they finally experience coherence?

They say: I feel like myself again.

They say: I did not know I was allowed to be this person everywhere.

They say: I am not as tired as I used to be.

They say: I finally know who I am---and I am not afraid to show it.

This is what integration produces. Not perfection. Freedom. Not the absence of struggle. The presence of clarity. Not a life without adaptation. A life without erasure.

This is what I want for you.

If this book has surfaced something in you—clarity, questions, hunger for more—I invite you into deeper work. Integration is not meant to be done alone. The I^3 framework is powerful, but it is most powerful when guided, when witnessed, when held in relationship with someone who can see what you cannot see in yourself.

For individuals who are ready to explore what integration could look like for your leadership and your life, I invite you to schedule a discovery call with me. This is not a sales conversation. Our conversation will be a genuine exploration of where you are, what you are navigating, and what might serve you. From there, we can create a plan unique to you and your journey.

You can also take the I^3 Leadership Integration Assessment, the diagnostic tool I've referenced throughout this book. It will give you a clear picture of where you are strong, where you are strained, and where your integration work needs to focus.

For leaders of organizations, if you lead an organization that is expanding globally, navigating cultural complexity, or seeking to develop leaders who can thrive across environments, Authentigrate offers training for your executives, your leaders, and your teams. I assist companies to prepare for, engage with, and retain global talent by equipping them with the tools to integrate authentically and to create successful transitions while increasing productivity, and protecting investment.

Please go learn more at authentigrate.com or authentigrate.ai.

Whatever you do next—on your own or alongside someone with expertise—do it intentionally. This is intentional work. It requires commitment, not just curiosity. It asks you to show up for yourself, for your leadership, for the people who need you to be whole.

Before I close this book, I want to speak something over you.

Cindy Trimm, Ph.D., my mentor, once wrote words about me that I carry as a reminder of who I am called to be. She called me a "noble joy-bringer" and saw me as someone who'd been raised to heal culture, amplify voices, and build systems rooted in soul wellness. She said I was "...named to name others, known to help the forgotten be known, and crowned to release crowns."

I receive those words. And I want to extend similar thoughts to you.

You are more than a leader. You are a carrier of something significant. The identity you have been excavating, the influence you have been elevating, the integration you have been practicing are professional assets as well as gifts meant to be given.

When you show up as the same person everywhere, you give others permission to enjoy that same kind of freedom. When you refuse to fragment, you create space for coherence around you. When you lead from identity rather than for approval, you model a different way of being in the world.

You have been named. You have been shaped. You have been prepared.

Now go and live it.

I want to close this reading experience you've had with a prayer for you—for wherever you are in your life, whatever your faith happens to be, and for whatever your journey has held.

May you become all that you were created to become.
May you live on purpose, with intention, in alignment.
May you never lose any part of yourself in the pursuit of belonging.
May you honor the identity that was given to you before you had words for it.
May your influence flow from your identity rather than your performance.
May you show up as the same person everywhere—coherent, aligned, and whole.
And may you know, deeply and truly, that you are not alone in your work.
Amen.

And now, be the same person everywhere.

There is an ancient proverb that says: "A tree with strong roots laughs at storms." That is what I want for you. Roots so deep that the storms of transition, expectation, cultural pressure, and role demands cannot uproot you. Not because you are rigid—but because you are anchored. Not because you refuse to bend—but because you know where your center is and you always return there.

You have spent time with this book learning what it means to strengthen your identity, elevate your influence, and practice integration. You have excavated who you are beneath the roles. You have learned to steward your presence without shrinking yourself. You have discovered that adaptation and authenticity are not opposites, and that you can honor the capacity of any room without abandoning your core.

Now the work is yours. Not as a burden. As an invitation.

You get to live integrated. You get to be the same person in every room you enter. You get to lead from identity rather than for approval. You get to belong without being erased.

This is your I^3 life. And it is waiting for you. Go and live it. The world needs the leader you are becoming. And that leader—whole, coherent, integrated—is already inside you.

A Final Declaration

I am not my roles. I am not my performance. I am not the versions of myself I created to survive. I am who I was made to be---before expectation, before fragmentation, before the world told me to shrink. I will strengthen my identity. I will elevate my influence. I will practice integration. I will be the same person everywhere. And I will help others do the same.

APPENDIX A
THE I^3 LEADERSHIP INTEGRATION SNAPSHOT

This brief assessment is designed to give you a starting point for reflection. It is not diagnostic. It is directional. Use it to notice patterns, not to assign labels.

For each statement, rate yourself on a scale of 1 to 5:

1 = Rarely true

2 = Sometimes true

3 = Often true

4 = Usually true

5 = Almost always true

IDENTITY

1. I know who I am independent of my roles and titles.

   1 2 3 4 5

2. I can articulate my core values without hesitation.

   1 2 3 4 5

3. My sense of self remains stable when I change environments.

   1 2 3 4 5

4. I do not need external validation to feel confident in who I am.

   1 2 3 4 5

5. I can distinguish between what I believe and what I was taught to believe.

   1 2 3 4 5

Identity Subtotal: _____ / 25

INFLUENCE

6. I lead from conviction rather than seeking approval.

   1 2 3 4 5

7. I can use my voice in rooms where I am outnumbered.

   1 2 3 4 5

8. I understand how my presence affects the environments I enter.

   1 2 3 4 5

9. I do not shrink my leadership to make others comfortable.

   1 2 3 4 5

10. I can advocate for my ideas without apologizing for them.

    1 2 3 4 5

Influence Subtotal: _____ / 25

INTEGRATION

11. I show up as the same person across different contexts.

    1 2 3 4 5

12. I do not feel like I am performing a version of myself at work.

    1 2 3 4 5

13. I can adapt my communication style without changing my values.

    1 2 3 4 5

14. I do not feel exhausted from managing different identities.

    1 2 3 4 5

15. People who know me in different contexts would recognize the same person.

    1 2 3 4 5

Integration Subtotal: _____ / 25

SCORING YOUR SNAPSHOT

Total Score: _____ / 75

60 to 75: Integrated Leadership. You have a strong foundation. Your work is refinement and expansion.

45 to 59: Emerging Integration. You have clarity in some areas and fragmentation in others. Focus on the pillar with the lowest score.

30 to 44: Active Fragmentation. You are likely experiencing the strain of managing multiple versions of yourself. This book will help you.

Below 30: Survival Mode. You may be disconnected from your core. Start with identity work before moving to influence or integration.

For the full I3 Leadership Integration Assessment with detailed reporting, visit authentigrate.com.

APPENDIX B
I^3 GLOSSARY OF TERMS

Anchored Identity — A sense of self that remains stable across environments, roles, and transitions. The opposite of adapted identity.

Adapted Identity — A self-constructed primarily through response to external expectations. Often mistaken for emotional intelligence or professionalism.

Capacity of the Room — The ability of an environment to receive your full presence. Some rooms have high capacity; others require you to calibrate your expression without abandoning your core.

Code-switching — The practice of shifting language, tone, behavior, or presentation across social and cultural environments. Necessary at times; costly when it becomes identity.

Discernment — The capacity to perceive what is happening beneath the surface in a room, a relationship, or a decision. Essential for strategic influence.

Fragmentation — The internal experience of living in disconnected versions of yourself across different environments. Often rewarded before it becomes costly.

I^3 Framework — A leadership formation model consisting of three pillars: Identity, Influence, and Integration. Designed to help leaders become the same person everywhere.

Identity — Who you are beneath roles, expectations, and performance. The foundation of the I3 framework.

Influence — How your presence, voice, and authority are experienced across environments. Leadership that flows from identity rather than performing for approval.

Integration — The capacity to live and lead as the same person everywhere. The culminating practice of the I3 framework.

Lethal Loyalty — Commitment to a person, organization, or role that requires you to sacrifice your identity to maintain belonging. A form of costly adaptation.

Role Compression — The experience of having your identity reduced to fit a single role or expectation. Happens when systems or relationships cannot hold your complexity.

Role Fusion — The merging of identity with a role to the point where the role becomes who you are. Common among high-capacity leaders who over-identify with their work.

Same Person Everywhere — The I³ definition of integration. Means you authentically show up, not assimilate, not dim your light, no identity loss.

ACKNOWLEDGMENTS

No book is written alone, and this one certainly was not.

To my husband, Dr. Tyrone Partee, who has walked with me through 17 years of becoming. You have seen me fragment and watched me integrate. You have held space when I could not hold myself. You are my evidence that wholeness is possible within relationship. Thank you for choosing me, again and again.

To my mother, Patricia, who taught me that protection and tenderness can live in the same body. You were my first example of a woman refusing to shrink. Everything I know about standing begins with you.

To my grandmother and grandfather, Lillian and Johnny Ballard, who showed me quiet strength is still strength. You sewed my first cheerleading outfit, never spoke an ill word about anyone, and your steady presence anchored my earliest sense of self.

To Reverend Cynthia James, Ph.D. my bishop, pastor, friend, and spiritual mother. You have poured into me in ways I am still discovering. Your voice echoes through these pages even where your name doesn't appear. Thank you for seeing what I could become before I could see it myself.

To Pastor Wayne Jackson, who recognized my calling as you prayed for my husband when I didn't yet know who he was. Your prophetic investment in my life continues to bear fruit.

To Ann Height, my business advisor and mentor, your strategic wisdom has shaped how I build. You model what it means to lead with both excellence and integrity.

To every leader who trusted me with your fragmentation, you let me witness your excavation. You showed me what integration looks like in real time. This framework exists because you were willing to do the work.

Authentically, and with love,
Alicia Partee

ABOUT THE AUTHOR

Alicia Partee, D. Min., M.A., has spent over three decades at the intersection of leadership, identity, and cultural integration as a Fortune 500 technology executive, licensed marriage and family therapist, transformational coach, and ordained minister.

Her own experience of fragmentation came into sharp focus in 2013, when she followed her husband to Norway and found herself navigating a world that could not read her. That season of rebuilding her sense of self from the ground up became the catalyst for the I^3 framework.

Today, Alicia is the CEO and Founder of Authentigrate, a data driven global mobility firm that helps organizations prepare, engage, and retain international talent. Through predictive analytics, AI powered cultural navigation, and personalized transition support for expatriates and their families, Authentigrate reduces assignment failure and protects organizational investment in global talent.

Alicia also serves as Executive Pastor and Chief of Staff at Bay Area Maranatha Christian Center.

She and her husband, Dr. Tyrone Partee, have six children and five grandchildren. They live in the San Francisco Bay Area. NOTE: About Tyrone's degrees, let's talk about what we did for him before and how he wants to show up in this book with the degrees he earned.

Learn more at authentigrate.com

Education

Doctor of Ministry, Spirit-Filled Global Leadership in the African Diaspora, Portland Seminary

Master of Arts, Marriage and Family Therapy, Western Seminary

Bachelor of Science, Theology and Leadership, William Jessup University

CONNECT WITH ALICIA PARTEE

You close the book. Maybe you are sitting with a cup of coffee. Maybe you are staring at your leadership role, your calling, your next chapter and asking a quiet question.

Who am I becoming as I lead?

That question is the heart of the I^3 journey. Identity. Influence. Integration.

If something in these pages stirred you, challenged you, or helped you name what you have been carrying, I would be honored to stay connected with you as you continue the work.

Start With Your Leadership Snapshot

Every leader is somewhere on the integration journey. Some are discovering their voice. Some are navigating cultural or organizational transitions. Some are leading while still asking where they truly belong.

The I^3 Leadership Snapshot will help you identify where you are right now and name your next step in leadership integration. Scan the code below or visit:

aliciapartee.com/i3

Stay Connected

Leadership is not a solo journey. It grows through reflection, conversation, and community. At aliciapartee.com you will find leadership insights and resources, speaking updates and new research, tools for navigating identity, belonging, and leadership transitions, and upcoming projects and writings.

aliciapartee.com

Bring Alicia to Your Organization or Event

Alicia speaks globally on leadership integration, cultural intelligence, identity formation, and thriving through transition. Her work bridges faith, leadership, psychology, and global culture, equipping leaders to show up as the same person everywhere. She is available for keynotes, leadership retreats, executive sessions, conferences and panels, and podcast and media interviews.

For booking inquiries, reach out at:
info@authentigrate.com

Leadership integration is not about becoming someone new.
It is about becoming fully who you are called to be.

So take the next step. Take the assessment. Reflect on where you are. Then lead forward with clarity.

You do not have to choose between who you are and where you are going.

Integration means you carry both.

ALSO BY DR. ALICIA PARTEE

AUTHENTIGRATE: An Ultimate Handbook to Navigate New Cultures

2022

A field guide for global sojourners navigating cultural transition. A practical and soulful companion for the journey toward true integration abroad.

30-Day Journey: A Christ-Centered Christmas

2023 | With Dr. Tyrone Partee

A daily devotional for the Advent season that slows the rush and recenters the celebration. Thirty days of spiritual practice for families and individuals.

My Fluffy Hair

2019

A children's picture book celebrating the beauty of natural hair and the confidence that comes from knowing who you are.

Mitt Lodné Hår

2019 | Norwegian Edition

The Norwegian edition of My Fluffy Hair, born from Alicia's years living in Norway and her commitment to belonging for children across every culture.

Available on Amazon.

Thank you!

Alicia Partee
AUTHENTIGRATE

www.ingramcontent.com/pod-product-compliance
Lightning Source LLC
LaVergne TN
LVHW010619100826
845148LV00014B/3032

* 9 7 9 8 9 8 5 6 6 6 3 6 6 *